By Klaus Wöckinger

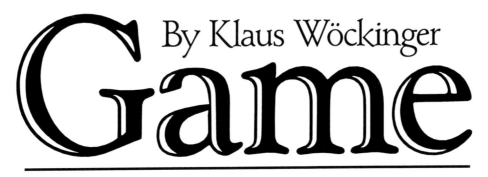

Game

The art of preparation and cooking
of game and game fowl

Published by N and C Publishing

To my wife Carole, K. W.

Canadian Cataloguing in Publication Data

Wöckinger, Klaus
    Game: the art of preparation and cooking of game and game fowl

2nd ed.
Includes index.

1. Game (Cookery).   1. Title.
TX751.W63   1992   641.6'91   C92 - 090659 - 1

Published in 1988 by N and C Publishing
Box Number 78062, H.P.O.
Calgary, Alberta
T2H 2Y1

ISBN 0 - 9693653 - 1 - 4 (hardcover)
ISBN 0 - 9693653 - 0 - 6 (paperback)
ISBN 0 - 9693653 - 2 - 2 (paperback)

1st Printing, 1988   2nd Printing, 1992

Design: Kay McKellar
Production: Rob Melbourne and Kitty McLeod
Photographs: Douglas Leighton
Proofreader: Susan Ranger
Color: United Graphic Services Limited
Typesetting: Foy and Flanigan
Printed in Canada: Ronalds Printing

TABLE OF CONTENTS

ACKNOWLEDGMENTS

The most important part of this book is the group of people who made it possible. I would like to thank in particular: Kay McKellar, Douglas Leighton, Susan Ranger, Josef deAngelis, Yvonne Inwood and Dr. and Mrs. J. B. Dundas for their great support during the entire project.

Acknowledgement is gratefully extended to the following businesses for the use of their props: Anne Paterson's Flowers, Plant Company, Marcel De Paris, Glass Haus-Dinnerware Studio, Trifles Lamps and Accessories Ltd., June Dyson Antiques.

My most sincere thanks go to all those people who contributed to this book lending their props, testing recipes and giving helpful suggestions.

Finally, my deepest appreciation goes to Carole, my wife. She has contributed literally hundreds of hours, enthusiasm and hard work. Without her support this book simply would not exist.

PREFACE

In my native Austria and throughout Europe, game meat is a much prized, seasonal delicacy. Centuries of tradition have contributed to the evolution of the art of game preparation for the table. Hunting in many countries is a rare privilege earned by those who devote much of their energy to the careful management of game habitats.

When I moved to Calgary, in the foothills of the Canadian Rockies, imagine my joy at discovering the opportunities for hunting, and the abundance, variety and accessibility of game. Here and throughout North America, are the ingredients to excite the palate of even the most discriminating diner.

Following this discovery, I hunted frequently during the hunting season with my family's table in mind. Because game freezes so well, each autumn's harvest keeps us feasting throughout the year. My wife Carole and I enjoy entertaining at home, and virtually all our dinner parties feature game dishes. We have had many guests who share our love of game but we have also hosted many who do not — or thought they did not — care for game. The responses of the latter have prompted much lively after-dinner discussion, and this book is the response to the many challenges and comments explored during those enjoyable evenings.

A long and meticulous process, the preparation of this book has been a much bigger job than I imagined. I selected recipes ranging from very simple to challenging — all of which can be prepared in your kitchen with readily available ingredients. Introducing helpful ideas and techniques borrowed from the professional kitchen, all recipes were tested repeatedly, first at home, then later by many friends and neighbors. My desire in writing this book was to show that game can be prepared and presented in the same way as domestic meat, resulting in most interesting dishes and thus dispelling misunderstandings regarding game cookery. If I am successful in this, I will be well rewarded.

Klaus Wöckinger
CALGARY, 1988

INTRODUCTION

The eating of game and game birds offers a distinctive, natural adventure for the palate. The mild "beefy" taste and texture of moose, the smooth rich flavor of a grain fed goose or the sage flavored antelope so tender you can cut it with a fork. Each individual game animal has a flavor which is unique and reminiscent of the area in which it lived.

With a little basic knowledge the cooking of game is quite simple. The preparation of the meal begins far from the kitchen. It begins in the field with the choice of quarry — diet and habitat — its age and sex, behavior, method of taking, handling in the field, aging, butchering and freezing. Once these factors, which contribute to the final product, are understood and dealt with accordingly, game dining is a delightful treat.

Because modern agribusiness carefully controls the lives and diets of domestic livestock, their meats have a constant flavor to which we have become accustomed. By contrast, different game animals living in different habitats have varying diets, giving variety of flavor to the meat. Meat from a deer feeding on a farmer's field will taste quite different from a high country deer feeding on native browse. Game is a natural food in every sense of the word.

This book invites you to explore the many possibilities of game cooking. Included are 128 recipes, many with pictures, for game and game birds, sauces, complementary dishes and desserts. All of these were tested repeatedly over the last two and half years, first at home then later in the kitchen of friends and neighbors. Many of them overcoming previously held misconceptions while delighting in the simplicity of game cooking. From those recipes the author has created ten menus, with full color pages, for your dining entertainment. Showing how to use color, meat carving and garnishes to improve the appearance and enhance the appetite. In addition the book has helpful basic guidelines, serving suggestions and substitutes. All the different game species have individual chapters for easy reference. In the ground meat chapter, complete instructions for sausage making can be found along with recipes using leftover meat. There is also a butchering section with detailed and picture-illustrated information on meat cutting, preparation and freezing.

For those who do not hunt or are not lucky enough to receive meat from friends who do, many game species (especially birds) are now raised commercially and are available for your table from specialty meat stores and a few supermarkets. If game meats are entirely unavailable to you, over 80 per cent of the recipes included in this book may easily be applied to the cooking of domestic meats such as beef, veal, lamb, pork, turkey, chicken, goose, duck and rabbit.

BASIC GUIDELINES

Marinating: One of the commonest misconceptions about game is that it must be marinated to improve its flavor. Marinating can enhance or moderate the flavor of some game, but a marinade can easily overwhelm the delicate flavor of the best of all game meats — prime young animals.

Preparation: Flouring steaks, medallions, schnitzels or piccatas will give a crusty coating which keeps meat juicy. Also, flour left in the pan will help thicken any accompanying sauce.

Pounding meat (schnitzel and piccata) will not only give a thin piece of meat which was thickly cut, it also breaks the meat fibre and so tenderizes meat. For example, in order to tenderize tough steaks pound them into schnitzels. Pounding between two sheets of plastic wrap will prevent meat from breaking into pieces and splattering.

Meat should be salted just before cooking. If meat stands after salting, moisture will be pulled to the surface of the meat making it difficult to brown. However, if meat is salted after cooking, the salt flavor will not penetrate the meat, making meat taste salty on the outside and bland on the inside.

Cooking: Use olive or peanut oil with butter when frying. These oils can take a higher frying temperature than other oils. Butter, which will easily burn if used alone, gives good flavor to fried meat. Using them in combination gives the advantage of both.

Because game meat is lean and can dry out easily, it should be seared first on a high heat to seal in the juices before the heat is lowered to finish the cooking. With the exception of bear and wild boar, game meat should be cooked until it is pink — medium rare to medium — for the best results.

In order to prevent juices from escaping, avoid puncturing the meat with a fork as you turn it. For the same reason, never carve game roasts immediately after removing from the oven. Instead, let the roast stand for 5 to 15 minutes to allow the juices to diffuse evenly.

It is very difficult when roasting a whole bird to keep breasts juicy and a little pink and, at the same time, have the legs cook to the well-done stage. Roast birds on their sides to protect breasts from hotter top heat in the oven.

Testing steaks or medallions for desired doneness is a difficult task, which requires experience. The time of frying will depend on the thickness and tenderness of the meat cut. Press meat with a finger or the back of a teaspoon; the harder the meat feels, the more the meat is done. Until experience is gained, cut steaks or medallions in the middle to judge doneness.

When adding wine to sauce, do not worry about alcohol content, the alcohol will evaporate within a few minutes during cooking leaving only the flavor. Madeira wine is often used in these recipes; if it is not available mix two-thirds port wine with one-third brandy.

Time saver: Time can be saved if pot roasts, stews or meat sauces are cooked in large quantities. After cooking these dishes, they may be refrozen for up to six weeks without any loss of quality.

Equipment: Cast iron cookware or a frying pan with ovenproof handles make it easy to work from stove to oven. This method is often used in the recipes in this book.

Wines: The right wine can enhance your game dining enjoyment. Red wines are generally preferred for most big game and game birds. However, white wines can be served with many game birds, or game served with cream sauces. There are no absolute rules. In general, choose a wine robust enough to complement the flavor of the meat and its sauce. Choose a hearty red wine for a deer roast served with a rich sauce, or a light white wine for delicate quail or partridge.

7

SOUPS, SAUCES AND MARINADES

SOUPS AND SAUCES

The juicy, lean perfection of game meat is enhanced greatly when served with a flavorful sauce. Sauces should be prepared and served to complement, rather than overwhelm, the flavor of the meat. Trimmings and bones from big game and carcasses of game birds can yield a delicious stock for sauces and soups. Sweet-tart jellies, such as cranberry or currant, are excellent and traditionally served with game dishes.

MARINADES

Young and good quality game meat should not be marinated, the fine flavor would be destroyed.

A marinade will tenderize and moderate or change the flavor of strong-tasting game meat.

Game Stock

for 3 L (12 cups)

1.5 kg (3 lbs) game bones and meat trimmings
4 Tbsp oil

1 medium onion, coarsely chopped
1 carrot, coarsely chopped
1 parsnip, coarsely chopped
2 cloves garlic
4 L (16 cups) cold water
1/2 tsp thyme
3 bay leaves
10 juniper berries
20 peppercorns
1 Tbsp salt

Preheat oven to 230°C (450°F). Chop bones and place with trimmings and oil in a roasting pan. Put in the oven to roast for 30 minutes.

Lower oven temperature to 200°C (400°F). Stir in the vegetables and garlic, roasting for another 20 minutes. Remove pan from the oven and transfer browned bones and vegetables with a slotted spoon into a large saucepan. Discard frying oil. Pour in sufficient water to cover bottom of the roasting pan and place back in the oven for 5 to 10 minutes. Remove from the oven and scrape off all solids from the bottom of the pan, using a wooden spoon. Pour this liquid over browned bones in the saucepan. This will give the stock a nice brown color. Add the remaining cold water to the bones and slowly bring to a boil. When stock is just about to boil, turn heat down and simmer stock. (This will keep it clear.) Skim foam from the top. Add all herbs, peppercorns and salt; simmer for 2 to 3 hours, skimming occasionally. Remove bones and vegetables carefully with a slotted spoon before straining stock through a cheesecloth. Cool at room temperature, then place in the refrigerator.

Note: Use this stock as a base for sauces and soups. Keeps 4 to 5 days in the refrigerator or freeze in small plastic containers.

Game Bird Stock

For game bird stock, follow same method as game stock, using bird carcasses, and adjust ingredients depending on the amount of bones available.

Note: When using a carcass from a roasted bird, fry vegetables in a large saucepan until soft. Add carcass and water, bring to a boil; add herbs and simmer for 2 to 3 hours.

Basic Game Sauce

about 1 L (4 cups)

1.5 kg (3 lbs) game bones and meat trimmings
4 Tbsp olive oil

2 Tbsp tomato paste
1 medium onion, coarsely chopped
1 medium carrot, coarsely chopped
1 medium parsnip, coarsely chopped
2 cloves garlic
1/2 orange, unpeeled
2 bay leaves
1/2 tsp thyme
1/2 tsp rosemary
25 peppercorns
10 juniper berries
80 mL (1/3 cup) flour
250 mL (1 cup) dry red wine
1.5 L (6 cups) water
1 tsp salt

Preheat oven to 230°C (450°F). Chop bones very small and place with trimmings and oil in a heavy roasting pan. Place in the oven to roast for 30 minutes, stirring occasionally.

Stir in tomato paste and roast for 10 minutes more. Lower oven temperature to 200°C (400°F). Stir in the vegetables, garlic, orange, herbs and flour and roast for another 20 minutes. Remove pan from the oven and transfer all the ingredients into a large saucepan. Pour wine into roasting pan and place back into the oven for 5 to 10 minutes. Remove from the oven and, with a wooden spoon, scrape off all solids from the bottom of the pan, then pour into saucepan. Set pan on the stove over medium high heat. Add 125 mL (1/2 cup) of the water and boil down until just dry, repeat this process one more time. (This will give the sauce a nice color. The steam will take all the flavor out of the bones and trimmings.) Add the remaining water and bring to a boil, stirring occasionally with wooden spoon. Add salt and simmer, uncovered, for 2 to 3 hours, stirring occasionally. Skim off the foam and oil which come to the top. Add water as necessary (liquid should stay at the same level). Remove bones with a slotted spoon and discard. Strain sauce through a fine sieve, pressing the vegetables to get their juices into the sauce. Bring back to a boil and reduce to a creamy consistency. Adjust seasoning with salt and pepper.

Note: Sauce will keep in the refrigerator for 1 week, if well covered, or pour into ice cube containers and freeze. Place cubes in a freezer bag. This way, the exact amount needed can be taken out.

This brown sauce is the base for many other sauces. Add cream and/or sautéed mushrooms and wines such as Madeira or port. Either reduce or thicken with cornstarch as necessary.

Substitute

If basic game sauce in not available, chop a small onion, carrot and celery and sauté in 1 Tbsp butter. When brown and soft, add 1 tsp tomato paste and 1 Tbsp flour. Fry a little longer and add 250 mL (1 cup) beef broth. Cook slowly for 30 minutes, then strain.

Basic Game Bird Sauce

For basic game bird sauce, follow same method as basic game sauce, using bird carcasses, and adjust ingredients depending on the amount of bones available.

Game Consommé

1 kg (2 lbs) lean game trimmings from shoulder, neck etc.
1 carrot
2 stalks celery
10 sprigs parsley
½ onion with peel

Grind meat with all the vegetables through the coarsest blade of a meat grinder.

4 egg whites
10 peppercorns, crushed
250 mL (1 cup) cold water
4 L (16 cups) cold game stock with no fat (see recipe, page 10)
Salt, pinch
Nutmeg, pinch

In a large saucepan, place egg whites, peppercorns and water, and mix well together. Add game stock and bring slowly to a gentle boil. Turn heat down and simmer for 1½ hours. (If consommé is allowed to boil too hard, it will become cloudy.) Strain consommé through cheesecloth and adjust seasoning with salt and nutmeg. (See picture, page 18.)

Serving suggestion

Garnish with julienne vegetables (very thin strips) such as celery and carrots or fine noodles, and sprinkle with chopped parsley or chives.

Substitute

Trimmings from game fowl and beef.

Cream of Wood Mushroom Soup

Serves 6

60 g (2 oz) dried wood mushrooms (bolets)
250 mL (1 cup) warm water

Method: Rinse sand from wood mushrooms quickly in cold water. Soak for 15 minutes in warm water, remove and chop coarsely. Reserve soaking water.

80 mL (⅓ cup) butter
2 Tbsp finely chopped onion
125 mL (½ cup) flour

Melt butter in a large saucepan over medium high heat. Add onion and mushrooms, and sauté for one minute. Stir in the flour and sauté for a further minute.

1 L (4 cups) game bird stock (see recipe, page 10) or chicken broth
125 mL (½ cup) whipping cream
2 Tbsp sherry (optional)
Salt and pepper, to taste
2 Tbsp chopped parsley

Pour in stock and reserved soaking water, and bring to a boil, stirring constantly. Turn heat down to medium and simmer for 30 minutes. Stir in the cream and simmer briefly. Add sherry (if used) and adjust seasoning with salt and pepper. If soup is too thick, thin with milk. Sprinkle soup with parsley when serving. (See picture, page 132.)

Spinach Soup

Serves 6

150 g (5 oz) spinach
2 Tbsp butter
1 small onion, chopped
1 L (4 cups) chicken broth
300 g (7 oz) potatoes, peeled and sliced
250 mL (1 cup) coffee cream
Salt and pepper, to taste
Nutmeg, pinch
1 Tbsp Pernod (optional)

Heat butter in a saucepan and sauté onion until soft but not brown. Add spinach and fry for a few more minutes. Pour in broth and add potatoes. Boil gently for 30 minutes. Place mixture into a blender or food processor and blend to a coarse texture. Return mixture to the saucepan and bring to a boil. Stir in cream and adjust seasoning with salt, pepper, nutmeg and add Pernod (if used). (See picture, page 70.)

2 slices white bread, cubed
1 Tbsp butter

Croutons: Fry bread cubes in butter until golden brown, and season with salt and pepper. When serving soup, sprinkle with the croutons.

Goulash Soup

Serves 6

500 g (1 lb) moose, elk or venison, from shoulder
3 Tbsp lard or oil
1 small onion, chopped
1 clove garlic, crushed
Salt and pepper, to taste
4 tsp Hungarian paprika
1½ Tbsp tomato paste
4 Tbsp flour
1.5 L (6 cups) beef broth
½ tsp marjoram
1 bay leaf
2 medium potatoes, peeled

Trim meat of ligaments and cut into 6 mm (¼ in.) cubes. Heat lard in a saucepan over medium heat. Fry onion and garlic until onion starts to turn brown. Season meat with salt and pepper and place with paprika and tomato paste into the saucepan. Fry for a few minutes. Add flour and stir thoroughly. Turn heat to medium high. Stir in 500 mL (2 cups) of the beef broth, bringing to a boil. Pour in the remaining broth; add marjoram and bay leaf. Simmer, partially covered, for 1¼ hours or until meat starts to become tender. Cube potatoes the same size as meat. Add to soup and simmer until meat and potatoes are tender. Soup should have a creamy consistency; otherwise, boil down or add water. Adjust seasoning with salt and pepper if necessary.

Serving suggestion

Serve soup as a full meal with crusty rolls.

Substitute

Beef.

13

Cold Cucumber Soup

Serves 6

500 g (1 lb) cucumbers
250 mL (1 cup) coffee cream
250 mL (1 cup) sour cream
250 mL (1 cup) plain yogurt
1/2 tsp salt
Pepper, freshly ground
125 g (4 oz) baby shrimps
1 Tbsp fresh dill weed or 1 tsp dry

Cut a few thin cucumber slices for garnish. Peel remaining cucumbers, cut in half lengthwise and remove all seeds. Blend with coffee cream in a blender or a food processor. Place in a bowl and mix in all the other ingredients, except shrimps. Chill for 1 hour. Chop shrimps coarsely and divide into 6 chilled soup cups. Pour soup on top and garnish with cucumber slices and dill weed. (See picture, page 36.)

Corn Chowder

Serves 4 to 6

500 mL (2 cups) chicken broth
1 L (4 cups) water
1 tsp salt
2 ears of corn
1 Tbsp butter
1/2 green bell pepper, diced
1/2 red bell pepper, diced
2 Tbsp chopped onion
250 mL (1 cup) coffee cream
5 Tbsp cornstarch
Salt and pepper, to taste

In a saucepan, bring broth and water to a boil. Add salt and ears of corn; boil slowly for 10 minutes. Remove corn and let cool. Pour broth into a bowl and set aside for later use.

Melt butter in a saucepan over medium heat. Add bell peppers and onion, and sauté until soft. Pour in broth and bring to a boil. With a sharp knife, cut corn kernels from cobs and add to the broth. Mix cornstarch with cream. Using a wire whisk, gradually stir cornstarch mixture into boiling broth until a creamy consistency. Adjust seasoning with salt and pepper. (See picture, page 8.)

Béarnaise Sauce

Serves 6

3 egg yolks
4 Tbsp dry white wine
250 g clarified butter (see Note)
Salt and pepper, to taste
1 tsp lemon juice
1 Tbsp chopped tarragon
1 Tbsp chopped parsley

Place egg yolks and wine into a large stainless steel bowl. Hold bowl on top of a pan of boiling water. Whisk ingredients in a back and forth motion until very thick and foamy. Mixture should be like a creamy mayonnaise. Remove bowl from steam and set on a damp cloth (so the bowl will not turn when stirring in the butter). Whisk in a round motion, adding WARM butter fat slowly. When stirring in butter fat, the sauce will thicken. If sauce gets too thick, add a few drops of hot water. Add salt, pepper, lemon juice, tarragon and parsley and stir until thoroughly mixed. Keep in a warm place before serving.

Serving suggestion

Excellent with any meat from the grill, whole roasted loin or tenderloin from big game.

Note: Melt butter using water bath or microwave oven. Do not use liquid from melted butter.

Hollandaise Sauce

For Hollandaise sauce, use the same recipe as béarnaise sauce, omitting tarragon and parsley.

Serving suggestion

Delicious with broccoli and asparagus. Pour over vegetables before serving.

Mushroom Sauce

250 mL (1 cup)

200 g (7 oz) mushrooms sliced
1 Tbsp butter
1 Tbsp chopped shallot or onion
3 Tbsp dry white wine
250 mL (1 cup) whipping cream
1 Tbsp flour
125 mL (1/2 cup) stock or broth
1 tsp Dijon mustard
1Tbsp chopped parsley
Salt and pepper, to taste

Heat butter over medium high heat. Sauté mushrooms and shallot for a few minutes. Deglaze pan with wine and reduce until just dry. Mushrooms should be left in pan while deglazing. Pour cream into pan and bring to a boil. Mix flour with stock. Using a wire whisk, gradually stir flour mixture into boiling cream to thicken; Add mustard, parsley and and season to taste with salt and pepper. Boil gently for 15 minutes. Sauce should have a creamy consistency; otherwise, boil down or, if too thick, add water.

Serving suggestion

Serve with medallions, steaks or schnitzels.

Vinaigrette

250 mL (1 cup) olive or vegetable oil
1 tsp Dijon mustard
1 shallot
1/2 tsp sugar
1/2 tsp salt
Pepper, pinch
1 clove garlic (optional)
6 Tbsp good red wine vinegar
2 Tbsp port or sherry wine

Place oil, mustard, shallot, sugar, salt, pepper and garlic (if used) in a blender. Blend slowly while adding vinegar and port.

Transfer into a bottle and use as needed. Shake bottle well before using. Vinaigrette will keep for weeks at room temperature.

Buttermilk Marinade

For approximately 1.5 kg (3 lbs) meat

If fresh game flavor is too strong, use milk marinade. This will make the taste milder without changing the actual flavor and will also tenderize the meat. For big game meat, buttermilk is preferred. For game fowl use milk. Make sure meat is covered with marinade.

1 L (4 cups) buttermilk or milk
15 peppercorns, crushed
2 bay leaves, crushed

Place meat in a dish. Sprinkle with pepper and bay leaves and pour buttermilk over. Cover and marinate for 1 to 3 days. After marinating, rinse meat with cold water and pat dry.

Red Wine Marinade

For approximately 1.5 kg (3 lbs) meat

On older, stronger-tasting (rutting) game meat, a red wine marinade is usually used. This will change the taste and give it a full flavor. Make sure meat is covered with marinade.

700 mL dry red wine
2 Tbsp red wine vinegar
½ tsp thyme
15 peppercorns, crushed
2 cloves
10 juniper berries, crushed
1 small carrot, coarsely chopped
1 clove garlic (optional)

Rub meat with thyme, peppercorns and juniper berries. Place in a non-metal dish. Pour wine and vinegar over meat and add carrots, cloves and garlic. Marinate for about 24 hours.

After marinating, pat meat dry. (When using marinade for cooking, first bring to a boil, then skim top with a slotted spoon.)

Dry Herb Marinade

For approximately 1 kg (2 lbs) meat

Herb marinade is more a seasoning than a marinade — adding herb flavor to the meat. Use on steaks and roasts.

1 tsp thyme
1 tsp tarragon
Rosemary, pinch
4 Tbsp oil

Rub meat with herbs, place in a bowl and pour oil over. Turn meat a few times in the marinade, cover and place in the refrigerator for about 2 hours.

VENISON/DEER

Although the term "venison" is sometimes used for all game meats, particularly in Europe, in this book it refers specifically to meat from native white-tailed, black-tailed and mule deer. Most information will also apply to introduced species, such as fallow and sika deer.

Of all big game meats, the most extreme variation in flavor occurs in venison. This ranges from the fine grained and mild flavored meat of young animals to the coarse grained and strongly flavored meat of old animals. Meat from rutting animals is always stronger in flavor and, if not handled properly, will be too gamy to enjoy.

The hide should be left on during aging except for rutting animals. Under proper conditions, young deer should be aged for seven days, older and rutting animals up to fourteen days. In both cases, the tenderloins should be removed after only two to three days of aging to prevent them drying out.

Loins and hind legs provide the best meat cuts. The hind leg of a young animal can be roasted whole for an exceptional feast. The saddle of venison is a classic dish. The shoulder and various trimmings make great braising roasts, stews, ground meat and sausages.

Venison Medallions with Cherries and
Black Peppercorn Sauce

Serves 4

8 medallions from loin or leg,
90 g (3 oz) each
2 Tbsp olive or peanut oil
2 Tbsp butter
Salt and pepper, to taste
Flour

Heat oil and butter in a heavy bottomed frying pan over medium high heat. Season medallions with salt and pepper, dip into flour and shake off excess. Fry medallions to your liking. Remove meat, set aside on a plate to catch the juices and keep warm.

Sauce:
1 Tbsp red wine vinegar
80 mL (1/3 cup) port wine
160 mL (2/3 cup) game stock (see recipe, page 10) or beef broth
1 Tbsp cornstarch
1 Tbsp cold water
20 fresh pitted cherries (or canned)
1/2 tsp black peppercorns, crushed
Salt, to taste

Stir vinegar into pan, scraping off solids from the bottom. Boil until just dry. Add port and stock. Boil down liquid to half the volume. Mix cornstarch with water. Using a wire whisk, gradually stir in just enough cornstarch mixture to thicken sauce. Add the cherries and meat juices; reduce until sauce has desired consistency. Season with peppercorns and add salt if necessary.

Serving suggestion

Place medallions on warmed plates and pour sauce over meat. Serve with creamy fettuccine or spaetzle (see recipe, page 137).

Substitute

All the deer family and antelope.

20

Venison Shoulder in Cream Sauce

Serves 6 to 8

1 shoulder from a young deer, trimmed, about 1.5 kg (3 lbs)
5 Tbsp butter
Salt and pepper, to taste

Sauce:
1 small onion, finely chopped
10 juniper berries, crushed
125 mL (1/2 cup) dry white wine
375 mL (1 1/2 cups) whipping cream
2 Tbsp cranberry jelly
Salt, to taste
Pepper, freshly ground

Serving suggestion

Substitute

Preheat oven to 200°C (400°F). Place butter in a roasting pan and put in the oven. Rub deer shoulder with salt and pepper.

When the butter starts foaming, add the deer shoulder, onion and juniper berries. Roast for 30 minutes, basting occasionally, then lower oven temperature to 180°C (360°F). Pour wine into pan, cover and braise meat until tender, which will take about 2 hours (depending on the age of the animal). Add water if necessary (do not allow all liquid to evaporate). Remove roast, set aside and keep warm.

On the stove, pour cream and cranberry jelly into pan, scraping off solids from the bottom. Reduce to desired consistency and adjust seasoning with a little salt and a lot of freshly ground pepper.

Carve shoulder and arrange on a warmed platter. Pour a little sauce over the meat and serve the remaining sauce on the side. Complement with spaetzle (see recipe, page 137), roesti (see recipe, page 134) or fettuccine. A salad on the side is a nice touch for this dish.

Mountain sheep, lamb, antelope shoulder and braising cuts from all the deer family.

Venison Chops in Mushroom Sauce

Serves 4

8 chops, 125 g (4 oz) each
2 Tbsp olive or peanut oil
2 Tbsp butter
Salt and pepper, to taste
Flour

Sauce:
1 Tbsp butter
200 g (7 oz) mushrooms, sliced
1 shallot or 1 Tbsp onion,
finely chopped
4 Tbsp dry white wine
250 mL (1 cup) whipping cream
Salt and pepper, to taste
1 Tbsp French mustard

1 Tbsp chopped parsley (for garnish)

Serving suggestion

Substitute

Heat oil and butter in a heavy bottomed frying pan over medium high heat. Season chops with salt and pepper, dip into flour and shake off excess. Fry to a light pink. Remove meat, set aside on a plate to catch the juices and keep warm.

Add butter to pan and sauté mushrooms with the shallot for a minute or so. Pour wine into pan and boil down until just dry. Add the cream and reduce until sauce starts to thicken. (Do not boil down too much; otherwise, sauce will curdle.) Add meat juices and adjust seasoning with salt, pepper and mustard.

Arrange 2 chops on each warmed plate, pour sauce over meat and sprinkle with parsley. Noodles or roesti (see recipe, page 134) will complement this dish.

All the deer family, antelope, veal and pork chops.
(Fry pork chops until well done.)

Note: From large animals, only 1 chop of 200 g (7 oz) per person will be needed.

22

Venison Skewer

Serves 4

600 g (21 oz) tender meat from leg
or loin
1 Tbsp olive oil
1 green bell pepper
1/2 onion
3 slices bacon
12 mushrooms

4 Tbsp olive or peanut oil
Salt and pepper, to taste

Serving suggestion

Substitute

Cut meat, green pepper, onion and bacon into bite-sized pieces. Heat oil in a frying pan over medium heat. Sauté green pepper, onion and bacon until they are soft, remove and set aside.
To place on skewers, start with meat, then one piece of each: bacon, onion, green pepper and mushroom. Start over again until all meat is used. (Remember to start and finish the skewer with meat; otherwise, pieces will fall off during cooking.)

Heat oil in a large frying pan over high heat. Season skewers and fry to your liking, or brush with oil and place them on a very hot grill.

Serve with curried rice (see recipe, page 136) spooned onto the middle of warmed plates. Strip off skewer with a fork onto rice. A mixed salad will complement this dish.

Different types of meat such as beef, liver and chicken can be mixed, as long as they are tender.

Venison Skewer

Saddle of Venison with Port Wine Sauce

Serves 6

1 saddle, 2 kg (4 lbs)
2 Tbsp olive or peanut oil
2 Tbsp butter
Salt and pepper, to taste
Thyme, pinch

Sauce:
60 mL (¼ cup) port wine
250 mL (1 cup) basic game sauce
(see recipe, page 11)
Salt, to taste
Pepper, freshly ground

Serving suggestion

Substitute

Preheat oven to 230°C (450°F). Heat oil and butter in a heavy bottomed frying or roasting pan over medium high heat. Season saddle with salt, pepper and thyme. Brown saddle on meat sides and place in the oven, meat side up, for 15 minutes. Lower oven temperature to 190°C (375°F) and roast for another 20 minutes. Baste saddle every 10 minutes during cooking. Remove meat, set aside on a plate to catch the juices and keep warm.

Using the same pan, discard frying oil and place pan back on the stove. Deglaze pan with port, add game sauce and bring to a boil. Add meat juices and adjust seasoning with salt and a lot of freshly ground pepper.

Bring saddle to the table to carve in front of the guests. Pour a little sauce on warmed plates, place meat on top. Surround with poached half pears stuffed with cranberry jelly, mousse of carrots (see recipe, page 136) and spaetzle (see recipe, page 137).

Antelope saddle, mountain sheep or lamb saddle.

Venison Steaks from the Grill —
Marinated with Herbs

Serves 6

6 steaks from leg or loin

Marinade:
2 Tbsp dry white wine
5 Tbsp olive oil
1 tsp thyme
1 tsp tarragon
1 tsp chopped parsley

Salt and pepper, to taste

Serving suggestion

Substitute

Mix all the ingredients of the marinade together. Place steaks in a shallow dish and pour marinade over. Let stand for at least 2 hours, turning steaks once.

Remove steaks from the marinade and season with salt and pepper. Fry on a very hot grill to your liking.

Serve with baked potatoes and crisp salad with vinaigrette dressing (see recipe, page 16).

All the deer family, antelope, mountain sheep, lamb, chicken legs and/or breasts.

Venison Schnitzels with Wood Mushroom Sauce

Serves 4

8 schnitzels from leg, 90 g (3 oz) each
3 Tbsp butter
Salt and pepper, to taste
Flour

Pound schnitzels with a mallet between two sheets of plastic wrap. Heat butter in a heavy bottomed frying pan over medium high heat. Season meat with salt and pepper, dip into flour and shake off excess. Fry quickly on both sides. Place schnitzels on a plate to catch the juices and keep warm.

Sauce:
2 shallots, finely chopped
100 g (3 ½ oz) fresh wood mushrooms or 30 g (1 oz) dried (see Method, page 12)
4 Tbsp dry white wine
4 Tbsp port wine
125 mL (½ cup) basic game sauce (see recipe, page 11) or beef broth
125 mL (½ cup) whipping cream
Salt and pepper, to taste

1 Tbsp chopped parsley (for garnish)

Add the shallots and mushrooms to the pan (adding a little more butter if necessary), and sauté for a few minutes. Deglaze pan with wine and port and boil down liquid to half the volume. Add game sauce, cream and meat juices to the pan and reduce to a creamy consistency. Adjust seasoning with salt and pepper if necessary.

Serving suggestion

Place 2 schnitzels on each warmed plate, pour sauce over and sprinkle with parsley. Complement with pasta, roesti (see recipe, page 134) or rice.

Substitute

All the deer family, antelope, veal and pork schnitzels. If wood mushrooms are not available, use cultivated mushrooms.

Roast Leg of Venison in Red Wine Sauce

Serves about 10 to 12

1 hind leg from a young deer, trimmed,
2.5 kg (5 lbs)
Salt and pepper, to taste
3 Tbsp butter
3 Tbsp oil

Sauce:
1 medium onion, chopped
1 carrot, chopped
2 bay leaves
25 black peppercorns, crushed
1 tsp thyme
10 juniper berries, crushed
1 Tbsp tomato paste
4 Tbsp flour
60 mL (1/4 cup) brandy
250 mL (1 cup) dry red wine
500 mL (2 cups) game stock
(see recipe, page 10) or beef broth
4 Tbsp cranberry jelly
Salt and pepper, to taste

Serving suggestion

Substitute

Preheat oven to 230°C (450°F). Rub deer leg with salt, pepper and butter. Place meat and oil into a large roasting pan and put in the oven. Total roasting time will be 1 hour and 20 minutes. Roast for 30 minutes; lower oven temperature to 190°C (375°F) and roast for another 30 minutes, basting the meat occasionally.

Stir in all vegetables, herbs and tomato paste, roasting another 15 to 20 minutes. Remove meat and wrap in foil to keep warm.

On the stove, add flour and fry for 2 to 3 minutes. Deglaze pan with brandy and wine. Bring to a boil, stirring constantly. Boil down liquid to half the volume. Add stock, bring back to a boil and cook slowly for 25 minutes.

Strain sauce through a sieve, pressing vegetables to get all their juices into the sauce. Stir in cranberry jelly and adjust seasoning with salt and pepper if necessary. Remove foil and return meat to pan. Pour sauce over the meat and place back in the oven for 10 minutes to reheat. Baste once with sauce.

Carve roast against the grain. Arrange on warmed platter and serve sauce on the side. Serve with spaetzle (see recipe, page 137) or noodles and glazed carrots. Poached pears add a nice touch to this dish.

Leg of antelope, mountain sheep and tender roasts from all the deer family.

Braised Venison Roast

Serves 6

1.5 kg (3 lbs) pot roast from leg or
shoulder
5 Tbsp oil
Salt and pepper, to taste
Thyme, pinch

1 onion, coarsely chopped
1 carrot, coarsely chopped
1½ Tbsp tomato paste
2 Tbsp flour
2 bay leaves
2 cloves
1 cinnamon stick, 10 mm (½ in.) long
5 juniper berries
15 black peppercorns
125 mL (½ cup) dry red wine
250 mL (1 cup) beef broth or water.

Serving suggestion

Substitute

Preheat oven to 180°C (360°F). Heat oil in a heavy bottomed saucepan over medium high heat. Season meat with salt, pepper and thyme. Brown on all sides. Remove meat and set aside.

Turn heat down to medium and fry onion, carrot and tomato paste. Cover and stir occasionally. (This way the vegetables become nicely soft.) Add flour and all herbs and fry for a few more minutes. Deglaze pan with wine, scraping off all solids from the bottom, then pour in the broth. Sauce will appear very thick but will become thinner from roast giving its juices to the sauce. Return meat to the pan, cover and place in the oven. Roast should be tender in 1½ to 2 hours.

Remove meat from the pan. Strain sauce through a fine sieve, pressing vegetables to get all their juices into the sauce and stir. Adjust seasoning if necessary.

Slice roast against the grain, and pour sauce over. Complement with servietten knoedel (see recipe, page 138) and poached pears with cranberry jelly.

All the deer family, antelope, mountain sheep, lamb, beef and buffalo.

Note: For variety add 2 Tbsp cranberry jelly and 125 mL (½ cup) whipping cream to the completed sauce. In this case, serve the roast with spaetzle (see recipe, page 137) and carrots.

Venison Roast Wrapped in Beef Fat

Serves 6 to 8

1.5 kg (3 lbs) roast from top sirloin, round or inside (top) round
Salt and pepper, to taste
300 g (10 oz) beef fat

Preheat oven to 230°C (450°F). Season roast with salt and pepper. Cut beef fat into thin slices, wrap around roast and tie with kitchen string.

Place meat in roasting pan and put into the oven. After 20 minutes lower oven temperature to 190°C (375°F) and roast for another 45 minutes for medium-rare. Remove meat, set aside on a plate to catch the juices and keep warm for 15 to 20 minutes before serving.

Serving suggestion

Remove beef fat and cut roast into thin slices against grain. Arrange on warmed plates or platter and pour meat juices over meat. Complement with fried potatoes and fried mushrooms. Sprinkle with green onions.

Substitute

All the deer family, antelope, mountain sheep and buffalo.

Venison Steaks with Herb Butter Sauce

Serves 4

4 steaks cut from loin or leg, 200 g (7 oz) each
2 Tbsp peanut or olive oil
1 Tbsp butter
Salt and pepper, to taste
Flour

Heat oil and butter in a large frying pan over medium high heat. Season steaks with salt and pepper, dip into flour and shake off excess. Fry to your liking. Remove meat, set aside on a plate to catch the juices and keep warm.

Sauce:
4 Tbsp dry white wine
Thyme, pinch
Tarragon, pinch
1/2 Tbsp chopped parsley
1 small clove garlic, crushed
2 Tbsp butter, COLD

Discard frying oil. Pour wine and meat juices into the pan and add the herbs and garlic. Boil down liquid by half, leaving 2 Tbsp. Over high heat, lift one side of the pan and shake when adding pieces of COLD butter, so butter will combine with the liquid.

Serving suggestion

Place steaks on warmed plates and pour sauce on top.
Serve with home made French fries and green beans.

Substitute

All the deer family, antelope, mountain sheep, lamb, pork chops, buffalo and beef steaks. (Do not flour beef.)

Venison Piccata

Serves 4

12 small piccatas cut from leg, 60 g
(2 oz) each
Salt and pepper, to taste
Sweet basil, pinch
Flour
1 large egg, beaten
6 Tbsp dried breadcrumbs
3 Tbsp Parmesan cheese, grated

4 Tbsp vegetable oil
2 Tbsp butter

Garnish:
1 Tbsp butter
100 g (3½ oz) mushrooms, sliced
100 g (3½ oz) ham, cut into fine strips

Serving suggestion

Substitute

Pound piccatas with a meat mallet between two sheets of plastic wrap until very thin. Season with salt, pepper and a little sweet basil. Have three bowls: one with flour, one with the egg and one with a mixture of breadcrumbs and Parmesan cheese. First, dip meat into the flour and shake off excess. Second, dip into the egg. Third, coat with breadcrumbs and cheese mixture, pressing it on with hands (shake off excess).

Heat oil and butter in a large frying pan over medium heat. Fry piccatas on both sides to a golden brown. Remove meat, set aside and keep warm.

In the same frying pan, add butter and fry mushrooms and ham strips.

Green noodles will complement this dish. Place noodles on center of each plate, arrange 3 piccatas around the noodles and put garnish on top of noodles.

All the deer family, antelope, mountain sheep, lamb, veal and pork.

Venison Medallions with Madeira Sauce

Serves 4

8 medallions from loin or leg, 90 g
(3 oz) each
2 Tbsp olive oil
1 Tbsp butter
Salt and pepper, to taste
Thyme, pinch
Flour

Heat oil and butter in a large frying pan over medium high heat. Season meat with salt, pepper and thyme. Dip into flour and shake off excess. Fry medallions to your liking. Remove meat, set aside on a plate to catch the juices and keep warm.

Sauce:
4 Tbsp dry white wine
4 Tbsp Madeira wine
125 mL (1/2 cup) basic game sauce
(see recipe, page 11) or beef broth

Pour wine and Madeira into the pan and boil down liquid to half the volume. Add sauce and meat juices and reduce again until of desired consistency. (If beef broth is used, mix 1 Tbsp cornstarch with an equal amount of cold water. Using a wire whisk, gradually stir in cornstarch mixture to thicken sauce.)

Garnish:
100 g (3 1/2 oz) ham, cut in fine strips
1 Tbsp butter

Fry ham briefly with 1 Tbsp butter.

Serving suggestion

Place 2 medallions on each warmed plate, pour sauce on top and garnish with ham strips. Complement with spinach and pasta or mashed potatoes. For color contrast, add cherry tomatoes.

Substitute

All the deer family, antelope, mountain sheep, lamb and veal medallions.

31

Venison Stew in Red Wine

Serves 6

1.5 kg (3 lbs) stewing meat
5 Tbsp olive oil
Salt and pepper, to taste

4 slices bacon, cut into strips
1 tsp thyme
10 juniper berries
2 bay leaves
2 Tbsp tomato paste
4 Tbsp flour
2 Tbsp red wine vinegar
250 mL (1 cup) dry red wine
250 mL (1 cup) game stock (see recipe, page 10) or beef broth
3 Tbsp cranberry jelly
Salt and pepper, to taste

Serving suggestion

Substitute

Cut stewing meat into bite-sized pieces. Heat oil in a large heavy bottomed saucepan over medium high heat. Season meat with salt and pepper and brown on all sides. (Do one-third at a time.) Remove meat with a slotted spoon and set aside.

When all meat has been browned and removed, turn heat down to medium. Fry the bacon for a few minutes, then add thyme, juniper berries, bay leaves, tomato paste and flour, and fry for a few more minutes. Deglaze pan with wine vinegar and red wine. Bring to a boil, scraping off solids from the bottom. Add stock and meat with juices to the pan and bring back to a boil. Cover and simmer slowly for 2 hours or until the meat is tender. Stir occasionally and add water if necessary. Add cranberry jelly and adjust seasoning with salt and pepper if necessary.

Complement with servietten knoedle (see recipe, page 138) or noodles and carrots.

All the deer family, antelope, mountain sheep and lamb.

Note: For variety, add 125 mL (½ cup) whipping cream and/or 100 g (3½ oz) fried sliced mushrooms. Add at the end of cooking time.

Stewing meat can also be marinated in red wine (see recipe, page 17) for 24 hours. If marinade is used for cooking, bring first to a boil in a separate pan and skim top.

Émincés of Venison in Gin Sauce (Venison Flakes)

Serves 4

600 g (21 oz) tenderloin or loin
3 Tbsp peanut oil
Salt and pepper, to taste
1/2 tsp juniper berries, finely crushed

Cut loin into fine flakes. Heat oil in a large heavy bottomed frying pan over high heat. Season flakes with salt, pepper and juniper berries. Fry briefly in very hot oil on all sides. Remove meat and set aside on a plate to catch the juices.

Sauce:
1 Tbsp butter
1 shallot, finely chopped
200 g (7 oz) fresh bolet mushrooms, sliced or 30 g (1 oz) dried (see Method, page 12)
2 Tbsp gin
250 mL (1 cup) whipping cream
125 mL (1/2 cup) game stock (see recipe, page 10) or beef broth
1 Tbsp cranberry jelly
Salt and pepper, to taste

Turn heat down to medium, add butter and sauté shallot with mushrooms until soft. Stir in the gin; then add the cream and scrape off all solids from the bottom of the pan. Over medium high heat, boil down liquid to half the volume. Add stock, cranberry jelly and meat juices; reduce sauce to a creamy consistency. Adjust seasoning with a little salt and lots of pepper. Return meat to the pan and bring just to a boil. (Do not boil, or meat will get tough.) Remove from heat and serve or keep warm.

Serving suggestion

Serve with spaetzle (see recipe, page 137), roesti (see recipe, page 134) or noodles. A salad on the side would be a nice touch.

Substitute

All the deer family and pork. If bolet mushrooms are not available, use cultivated mushrooms.

Venison Liver with Onion and Apple

Serves 4

1 liver from young beast, cut into steaks, calculate 180 g (6 oz) per serving
1 Tbsp peanut oil
2 Tbsp butter
Flour
Salt and pepper, to taste

Garnish:
1 medium onion, sliced
1 large apple, peeled, cored and cut into strips

Serving suggestion

Substitute

Note:
Liver from animals up to 2 years old is delicious. From older animals, liver may need to be soaked overnight in milk. Liver from males during the rutting season is not edible. Always remove outer skin. This is easily done by forcing skin off liver with thumb. (See picture, page 165.)

Heat oil and butter in a non-stick frying pan over medium heat. Dip liver steaks into flour and shake off excess. Fry to a light pink. (Liver should not be overcooked; otherwise, it will become hard and dry.) Remove meat, season with salt and pepper, set aside and keep warm.

Add onion to the pan and fry until lightly brown and soft (adding a little butter if necessary). Add apple and fry for 1 more minute.

Arrange liver on warmed plates, and place the fried onion and apple on top. Serve with creamy mashed potatoes.

All the deer family, mountain sheep, lamb and calf liver.

Venison Liver with Onion and Apple

Quenelles of Venison Liver (Dumplings)

Serves 6 to 8

300 g (10 oz) liver
125 g (4 oz) beef suet
1 slice white bread
1 Tbsp milk
1 Tbsp butter
1 small onion, chopped
1 small clove garlic, crushed
4 sprigs parsley
1 tsp salt
1/2 tsp marjoram
Pepper, to taste
60 mL (1/4 cup) dried breadcrumbs

4 L (16 cups) water and 1 tsp salt
(approximately)

(For liver information see Note, page 34.)
Trim liver of skin and veins. Soak bread with milk. Heat butter in a frying pan over medium high heat. Sauté onion and garlic until soft and let cool. Grind liver, beef suet, onion, garlic, soaked bread and parsley through the finest blade of a grinder. Season this mixture with salt, marjoram, pepper and mix in the breadcrumbs. (The mixture should have a dough-like texture.)

In a large saucepan, bring salted water to a boil. Rinse hands in cold water and shape dumplings to a golf ball size; drop them in the boiling water as they are made. Simmer for 15 to 20 minutes.

Serving suggestion

Serve in a consommé or with stews.

Substitute

Beef and pork liver.

Note: Liver dumplings are often enjoyed by people who do not like liver. Cooked dumplings will keep for days covered in the refrigerator.

For variety, make larger liver dough balls, roll them in dried breadcrumbs, shape into patties and fry them slowly in butter. Serve with apple sauce.

MOOSE AND ELK

MOOSE

Of all big game, the texture and flavor of moose meat is the closest to beef. Many beef recipes can be used to prepare moose.

The hide should be removed before aging to cool the carcass quickly. Because the meat has a high water content, there will be few dehydration problems.

Under proper conditions, a young moose should be aged for about ten days, and old or rutting moose up to eighteen days. Front quarters need only to be aged for about five days, since this meat is more suitable for pot roasts, stews, ground meat and sausages. The tenderizing process for these cuts will be completed during the cooking or the preparation.

The loin sections and tender parts on the hind legs yield superb medallions, steaks and roasts.

ELK

Elk has a fine grained, mildly flavored meat which can be extremely tender in young animals.

The hide can be left on during aging, except for rutting animals. Under proper conditions, young elk should be aged for about ten days and old or rutting elk for up to eighteen days.

As with moose, elk front quarters need only to be aged for about 5 days, since this part of the animal is more suitable for pot roasts, stews, ground meat and sausages. The cooking or preparation completes the tenderizing process for these cuts.

Medallions, steaks and prime roasts can be cut from loin sections and tender parts from hind legs. Because elk meat has a low water content, it is ideal for making jerky, salami or for smoking.

37

Braised Moose Roast

Serves 6

1.5 kg (3 lbs) roast from outside (bottom) round or cuts from shoulder
3 Tbsp oil
Salt and pepper, to taste

1 large onion, coarsely chopped
1 carrot, peeled and coarsely chopped
1 clove garlic
2 bay leaves
1 Tbsp tomato paste
½ tsp thyme
125 mL (½ cup) dry red wine
250 mL (1 cup) game stock (see recipe, page 10) beef broth or water
Salt and pepper, to taste

Serving suggestion

Substitute

Preheat oven to 180°C (360°F). Heat oil in a heavy bottomed roasting pan over medium high heat. Season roast with salt and pepper. Brown on all sides. Remove meat and set aside.

Turn heat down to medium and fry vegetables, garlic and bay leaves until soft. Add tomato paste and thyme and fry slowly for another 5 minutes. Stir in wine, scraping off solids from the bottom of the pan. Stir in stock. Return roast to the pan, cover tightly and place in the oven. Cook until tender which will take from 2 to 3 hours, depending on the cut. Remove meat and discard bay leaves. Put the liquid with the vegetables into a blender and purée into a sauce. Reheat and adjust seasoning with salt and pepper if necessary.

Slice roast and arrange on warmed plates or platter. Pour sauce on top. Serve with pasta.

All the deer family, antelope, beef and buffalo.

Braised Moose Heart

Serves 4

500 g (1 lb) heart
2 Tbsp butter
Salt and pepper, to taste
2 slices bacon, cut into strips
2 Tbsp finely chopped onion

1 Tbsp flour
60 mL (1/4 cup) dry red wine
250 mL (1 cup) game stock (see recipe, page 10) or beef broth
Salt and pepper, to taste

Garnish:
2 Tbsp sour cream
1 Tbsp milk
1 medium sour pickle

Serving suggestion

Substitute

Cut moose heart into 6 pieces and trim off all the fat. Wash in cold water and dry with a paper towel. Heat butter in a saucepan over medium heat. Season heart with salt and pepper and sauté on both sides with bacon and onion. Remove heart and set aside.

Add flour to the pan and fry briefly. Stir in wine and scrape off solids from the bottom. Add stock and bring to a boil. Return heart to pan, cover and braise gently over low heat for 1 to 1 1/2 hours. Add water occasionally if sauce becomes too thick and adjust seasoning with salt and pepper.

In a bowl mix sour cream and milk together, set aside for later use. Cut pickle into fine strips and set aside.

Cut heart into thin slices and pour sauce over meat. Top with the sour cream and milk mixture and garnish with pickle strips. Complement with creamy mashed potatoes.

Beef, buffalo and elk heart.

Moose Goulash

Serves 4 to 6

1 kg (2 lbs) stewing meat
5 Tbsp lard or oil
Salt and pepper, to taste

Cut meat into bite-sized pieces. Heat oil in a large heavy bottomed saucepan over high heat. Season meat with salt and pepper. Brown on all sides; do in two batches. Transfer meat onto a plate with a slotted spoon.

4 medium onions, finely sliced
4 cloves garlic, chopped
2 Tbsp Hungarian paprika
4 bay leaves
1 tsp marjoram
1 Tbsp vinegar
250 mL (1 cup) game stock (see recipe, page 10) or beef broth

Turn heat down to medium. Add onions and garlic to the pan, stir thoroughly and cover. Simmer onions, stirring occasionally, for approximately 20 minutes or until they are soft. Return meat to the pan and add paprika, bay leaves and marjoram. Fry briefly. Pour in the vinegar, add half the stock and cover. Simmer gently. When nearly all liquid is evaporated, add the remaining stock. (Never cover the meat with liquid. Onions disintegrate completely if liquid is kept low.) Add water as necessary. Meat should be tender in 2 hours.

Serving suggestion

Serve goulash with spaetzle (see recipe, page 137), rice, pasta, boiled potatoes or crusty French bread.

Substitute

All the deer family, beef, antelope, mountain sheep, lamb, buffalo, pork, wild boar and bear.

Moose Steaks Braised with Onions and Beer

Serves 6

6 steaks from shoulder or outside (bottom) round, 200 g (7 oz) each
4 Tbsp butter
Salt and pepper, to taste

Preheat oven to 180°C (360°F). Heat butter in a large saucepan over medium heat. Season steaks with salt and pepper. Brown on both sides. Remove meat and set aside.

2 large onions, 500 g (1 lb), sliced
1 clove garlic, chopped
2 Tbsp flour
1 bottle beer (dark is preferable)
Thyme, pinch
Marjoram, pinch

Place onions and garlic in the pan and sauté until golden brown and soft. Stir in flour and fry for a minute. Add beer and bring to a boil, scrape off all solids from the bottom of the pan. Return meat to the sauce and add thyme and marjoram. Cover tightly and place in the oven. Meat should be tender in about 1½ hours.

1 Tbsp chopped fresh chives
(for garnish)

Remove meat, place on a serving dish and keep warm. Bring sauce back to a boil and adjust seasoning if necessary.

Serving suggestion

Pour sauce over steaks, sprinkle with chopped chives. Serve with mashed or boiled potatoes and carrots.

Substitute

All the deer family, beef, buffalo and lamb.

Moose Brisket in Vinaigrette

Serves 6 to 8

Broth:
1 brisket, 1.5 kg (3 lbs)
4 L (16 cups) water
1½ tsp salt
1 medium onion
1 medium carrot
1 stalk celery
1 medium leek (optional)
20 peppercorns
2 bay leaves
2 cloves

In a large saucepan, bring water to a boil. Add salt and brisket, bring back to a gentle boil. Skim foam off the top. Do not peel onion, cut in half and brown in a small frying pan over medium heat without any oil. This will give the broth a good flavor and nice color. Add onion with all the other ingredients to the broth. Simmer slowly for 2 to 3 hours or until meat is tender. Let cool to room temperature.

Vinaigrette:
3 Tbsp finely chopped onion
3 Tbsp finely chopped red bell pepper
½ tsp salt
Pepper, pinch
½ tsp sugar
4 Tbsp cider or wine vinegar
3 Tbsp olive oil
125 mL (½ cup) broth (use broth in which brisket was cooked)

1 Tbsp chopped fresh chives
(for garnish)

Mix all the vinaigrette ingredients together in a bowl.

Cut brisket, against the grain, into 3 mm (1/8 in.) thick slices. Arrange on a large deep serving dish and pour vinaigrette on top. Let marinate in a cool place for 1 hour.

Serving suggestion

Sprinkle with chives before serving. Serve with crusty French bread. (See picture, page 43.)

Substitute

Buffalo and beef brisket.

Note: The leftover broth makes an excellent soup. Strain and garnish with noodles. Adjust seasoning with salt.

Moose Brisket in Vinaigrette with Broth

Moose Rouladen in Red Wine Sauce

Moose Rouladen in Red Wine Sauce

Serves 6

Stuffing:
300 g (10 oz) any game meat
100 g (3 ½ oz) pork fat
1 slice white bread
1 Tbsp milk
Salt and pepper, to taste

Cut the bread crusts off and discard. Pour milk over bread and grind with game meat and pork fat. Season with salt and pepper, and mix thoroughly.

Rouladen:
6 steaks from leg, 150 g (5 oz) each
1 medium onion, finely sliced
1 Tbsp butter
1 Tbsp Dijon mustard
6 slices bacon

Preheat oven to 180°C (360°F). Pound steaks with a mallet between two sheets of plastic wrap until very thin. Sauté onion in butter until golden brown and soft. Lay steaks on the counter and brush with mustard, place bacon and fried onion on top. Spread on the ground meat, fold in the sides of the steak and roll up. Tie around crosswise with kitchen string or secure with toothpicks.

2 Tbsp olive oil
1 Tbsp butter
Salt and pepper, to taste

Heat oil and butter in a large saucepan over medium high heat. Season rouladen with salt and pepper. Brown on all sides. Remove meat, set aside on a plate to catch the juices.

Sauce:
1 Tbsp tomato paste
2 Tbsp flour
125 mL (½ cup) dry red wine
250 mL (1 cup) game stock (see recipe, page 10), beef broth or water
15 peppercorns
2 bay leaves
Thyme, pinch
1 tsp sugar
Salt and pepper, to taste

Turn heat down to medium. Add tomato paste and flour to pan and fry for 3 minutes. Stir in wine and scrape off all solids from the bottom of the pan. Pour in the stock, bring to a boil and add peppercorns, bay leaves, thyme and sugar. Return meat with juices to the pan. Cover and place in the oven. Meat should be tender in 1 to 1¼ hours. Place rouladen onto a serving dish and remove strings or toothpicks. Skim oil from the top of the sauce and bring back to a boil. Add water if sauce is too thick and adjust seasoning with salt and pepper. Strain sauce and pour over moose rouladen. (See picture, page 44.)

Serving suggestion

Serve with baked potatoes and colorful vegetables.

Substitute

All the deer family, antelope, buffalo and beef.

Note: For variety, add 2 Tbsp cranberry jelly and 125 mL (½ cup) whipping cream to sauce.

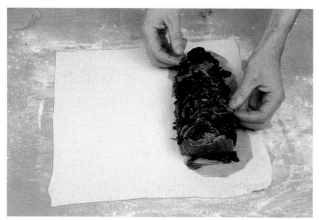

Place tenderloin on top of spinach and ham; cover with remaining spinach.

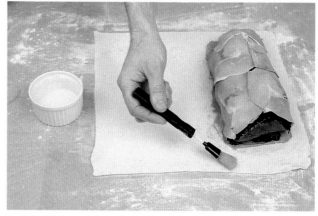

Brush edges of dough with egg wash.

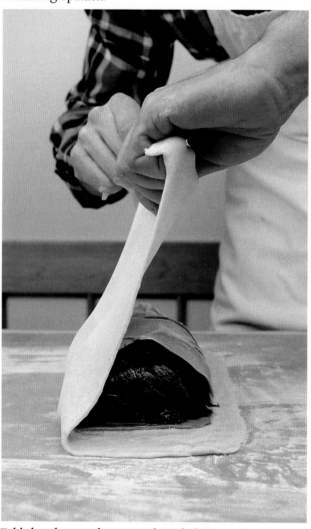

Fold dough over the covered tenderloin.

Poke dough with a fork.

46

Moose Tenderloin in Puff Pastry

Serves 6 to 8

Puff pastry dough:
500 g (1 lb) puff pastry dough

1.2 kg (2½ lbs) tenderloin
Salt and pepper, to taste
4 Tbsp olive or peanut oil
250 g (9 oz) spinach

Flour

10 slices of ham
1 egg yolk mixed with 1 Tbsp water

(For recipe, see page 151) or frozen commercial dough can be used.

Season tenderloin with salt and pepper. Heat oil in a heavy bottomed frying pan, brown meat on all sides in very hot oil. Remove meat, set aside and let cool. Wash spinach and blanch in salted boiling water for 2 minutes. Cool in ice cold water, drain and squeeze as much water as possible out of spinach and set aside.

Assembling: (See picture, page 46.)
Preheat oven to 200°C (400°F). On a floured surface, roll out the puff pastry to about a 3 mm (1/8 in.) thickness. (The pastry should be 20 mm (1 in.) longer than the loin and three times as wide.) Sprinkle a baking sheet with flour and shake off excess. Lay puff pastry on it.

Center 4 slices of ham along one end of the pastry, leaving a 10 mm (½ in.) border of dough uncovered to be pressed closed later. Spread one-third of the spinach on the ham and lay the tenderloin on top. Cover meat with the rest of the spinach and ham. To close the pastry, brush the edges with egg yolk mixture and fold the pastry over the meat. Trim away any excess pastry, then press edges together with a fork.

Brush pastry with egg mixture and poke it in several places with a fork to allow steam to escape while cooking. (Optional: decorate with remaining dough.) Bake for 25 to 30 minutes for medium rare. For medium, lower oven temperature to 175°C (350°F) and bake for an additional 10 minutes or 20 minutes for medium-well done. Let meat rest for at least 10 minutes in a warm place before slicing. While resting meat, cut off the two pastry ends to allow steam to escape and prevent further cooking of the meat. Tilt baking sheet to drain meat juices so pastry does not become soggy.

(Continue page 48.)

Madeira Sauce:
250 mL (1 cup) basic game sauce
(see recipe, page 11)
60 mL (¼ cup) Madeira wine
Salt and pepper, to taste

Bring game sauce with Madeira to a boil. Adjust seasoning with salt and pepper if necessary.

Serving suggestion

Place a little sauce in the middle of each warmed plate. Arrange two slices of meat on top. Surround with colorful vegetables. Serve extra sauce on the side.

Substitute

This recipe can be used with many types of meat such as well-trimmed veal, deer loin, elk, buffalo, beef tenderloin, mountain sheep and lamb loin.

Note: When using tenderloin or loin from smaller animals such as: deer, sheep or lamb, shorten baking time (e.g. lamb 15 to 20 minutes for medium rare).

Moose Roast in Aluminum Foil

Serves 6

1.5 kg (3 lbs) roast from leg or shoulder
100 g (3½ oz) pork back fat
Salt and pepper, to taste
1 tsp thyme
2 Tbsp olive oil
2 Tbsp butter

Preheat oven to 175°C (350°F). Lard roast (see Butchering). Season roast with salt, pepper and thyme. Heat oil and butter in a frying pan over medium high heat. Brown roast on all sides to a deep brown. Remove meat and set aside.

1 medium onion, finely chopped
1 clove garlic, crushed
2 bay leaves

Add onion, garlic and bay leaves to the pan and fry until golden brown and soft. Place roast onto 2 or more layers of aluminum foil (placed crosswise) and arrange onions on top of meat. Close foil tightly, set in a frying or roasting pan and place into the oven. Bake for 3½ to 4 hours.

Serving suggestion

Remove roast from foil, slice and arrange on warmed plates or platter. Pour onion and meat juices on top. Serve with creamy mashed potatoes and carrots or a salad on the side.

Substitute

All the deer family, antelope, mountain sheep, buffalo and beef.

Moose Steaks with Chive Sauce

Serves 4

4 steaks from loin or leg,
200 g (7 oz) each
2 Tbsp olive oil
2 Tbsp butter
Salt and pepper, to taste
Flour

Heat oil and butter in a heavy bottomed frying pan over medium high heat. Season steaks with salt and pepper, dip into flour and shake off excess. Fry to your liking. Remove meat, set aside on a plate to catch the juices and keep warm.

Sauce:
1 Tbsp finely chopped onion or shallots
80 mL (1/3 cup) dry red wine
125 mL (1/2 cup) beef broth
2 Tbsp COLD butter
1½ Tbsp chopped fresh chives

Discard frying oil, leaving 1 Tbsp. Fry onion without letting them get brown. Deglaze pan with wine and boil down liquid to half the volume. Pour in the broth and boil down, leaving 3 Tbsp of liquid. Break up the COLD butter and add with chives and meat juices to the pan. Boil briefly while shaking the pan back and forth so butter and liquid will combine into a sauce.

Serving suggestion

Place steaks on warmed plates and pour 1 Tbsp of sauce on each. Fried potatoes and green vegetables will complement this dish.

Substitute

All the deer family, antelope, buffalo and beef steaks. (Do not flour beef.)

Elk Schnitzel with Lemon

Serves 4

4 schnitzels from leg, 150 g (5 oz) each
Salt and pepper, to taste
2 eggs
Flour
250 mL (1 cup) dry breadcrumbs

Pound schnitzels very thin with a mallet between two sheets of plastic wrap. Season with salt and pepper. Beat the eggs with a fork. Dip both sides of the meat into flour and shake off excess, then dip into the eggs and last, into breadcrumbs.

4 Tbsp oil
4 Tbsp butter
1 lemon, cut into wedges

Heat oil and butter in a large frying pan over medium heat. Fry schnitzels on both sides to a golden brown. Remove meat and serve with a lemon wedge on top of the meat.

Serving suggestion

Excellent with mixed salad, beet salad, potato salad or mixed vegetables and potatoes or rice.

Substitute

Schnitzels from the deer family, pork, veal and turkey.

Elk Loin Roast in Port Wine Sauce

Serves 4 to 6

1 kg (2 lbs) roast from loin
2 Tbsp olive oil
2 Tbsp butter
Salt and pepper, to taste
1 tsp thyme

Preheat oven to 230°C (450°F). Heat oil and butter in a heavy bottomed frying pan over medium high heat. Season roast with salt, pepper and thyme, and brown on all sides. Put in the oven. After 15 minutes, lower oven temperature to 190°C (375°F). Baste meat with dripping. Roast for another 20 minutes for medium rare to medium. Remove meat, set aside on a plate to catch the juices and keep warm.

Sauce:
80 mL (⅓ cup) port wine
125 mL (½ cup) game
stock (see recipe, page 10) or beef broth
1 Tbsp cornstarch
1 Tbsp cold water
Salt and pepper, to taste

Using the same pan, discard frying oil and set pan back on the stove. Deglaze pan with port and stock and bring to a boil. Mix cornstarch with water. Using a wire whisk, gradually stir in cornstarch mixture to thicken sauce. Add meat juices to sauce and adjust seasoning with salt and pepper if necessary.

Serving suggestion

Carve roast into thin slices. Pour a little sauce on warmed plates and arrange meat on top. Serve with colorful vegetables and potatoes.

Substitute

All the deer family and mountain sheep.

Elk Steaks with Green Peppercorn Sauce

Serves 4

4 steaks from leg or loin, 180 g (6 oz) each
2 Tbsp olive oil
1 Tbsp butter
Salt and pepper, to taste
Flour

Heat oil and butter in a heavy bottomed frying pan over medium high heat. Season steaks with salt and pepper, dip into flour and shake off excess. Fry to your liking. Remove meat, set aside on a plate to catch the juices and keep warm.

Sauce:
1 shallot, finely chopped
2 tsp green peppercorns
2 Tbsp dry white wine
250 mL (1 cup) whipping cream
1 tsp Dijon mustard
Salt, to taste

Discard frying oil, leaving 1 Tbsp. Sauté shallot and green peppercorns briefly. Pour wine into the pan, boil down liquid to one-fourth and stir in cream and mustard. Reduce again until sauce becomes slightly thick. Add meat juices to the sauce. Adjust seasoning with salt if necessary.

Serving suggestion

Arrange steaks on warmed plates and pour sauce over. Serve with green vegetables and homemade French fries.

Substitute

Buffalo, beef (do not flour), pork chops, antelope, mountain sheep and all the deer family.

Braised Elk Roast

Serves 6

1.5 kg (3 lbs) roast from outside (bottom) round or cut from shoulder
Salt and pepper, to taste
3 Tbsp oil
1 large onion, coarsely chopped
1 clove garlic, crushed
300 mL (1¼ cups) light beef broth or water
1 large carrot, coarsely chopped
6 sprigs parsley

Serving suggestion

Substitute

Preheat oven to 180°C (360°F). Season meat with salt and pepper. Heat oil in a roasting pan over medium high heat. Brown roast on all sides. Remove meat and set aside. Turn heat down to medium and sauté onion and garlic until nicely brown. Pour broth into the pan and bring to a boil. Return meat to pan, add carrots and parsley, and cover.

Place in the oven for about 2 hours (if meat is very tough, it will take longer). Remove meat and set aside. Pour liquid and vegetables into a blender and purée into a sauce, then return sauce to the pot. Sauce should now have a nice consistency; otherwise, boil down or add liquid as needed. Adjust seasoning.

Cut roast into thin slices against the grain. Place into serving dish, pour a little sauce on top and serve the remaining sauce on the side. Sprinkle with chopped parsley. Complement with steamed potatoes and green beans or peas.

All the deer family, antelope, mountain sheep, beef and buffalo.

Braised Elk Roast (larded)

52

Braised Elk and Pork Ribs
Serves 4 to 6

1.5 kg (3 lbs) ribs, half elk and half
pork cut, 5 cm (2 in.) long
2 Tbsp peanut oil

Preheat oven to 230°C (450°F). Wash ribs in cold water and dry with a paper towel. Place oil and ribs into a large roasting pan and put in the oven. Brown meat for 30 to 40 minutes, stirring once.

Sauce:
3 Tbsp soya sauce
80 mL (1/3 cup) sherry
160 mL (2/3 cup) water
2 cloves garlic, crushed
1 Tbsp finely chopped fresh ginger
4 Tbsp brown sugar
1 Tbsp cornstarch
1 Tbsp cold water

Mix all the sauce ingredients except cornstarch, in a bowl.

Remove pan from the oven and skim off as much fat as possible. Pour sauce over meat, cover and return to the oven. Lower oven temperature to 180°C (360°F) and braise for 1 1/2 hours or until meat is tender. Remove meat with a slotted spoon, set aside in a serving bowl and keep warm.

Skim fat from the top of the sauce and bring to a boil. The sauce should amount to approximately 250 mL (1 cup); otherwise, add water or boil down. Mix cornstarch with water and gradually stir into sauce. Boil briefly, pour over ribs and mix thoroughly.

Serving suggestion

Serve with steamed rice.

Substitute

All the deer family and beef ribs.

Note: The reason for mixing pork and game ribs is for flavor and it also gives more meat since game ribs shrink considerably when cooked.

A wok can be used for this recipe. Brown ribs in hot oil, add sauce, cover and braise until tender. Finish sauce as mentioned above.

Elk Medallions with Wood Mushrooms and Madeira Sauce

Elk Medallions with Wood Mushrooms and Madeira Sauce

Serves 4

8 medallions from loin or leg, 100 g
(3 ½ oz) each
2 Tbsp olive or peanut oil
2 Tbsp butter
Salt and pepper, to taste
Flour

Heat oil and butter in a heavy bottomed frying pan over medium high heat. Season medallions with salt and pepper, dip into flour and shake off excess. Fry medallions to your liking. Remove meat, set aside on a plate to catch the juices and keep warm.

Sauce:
60 mL (¼ cup) dry white wine
60 mL (¼ cup) Madeira wine
125 mL (½ cup) game stock (see recipe, page 10) or beef broth
1 tsp cornstarch
1 tsp cold water

Deglaze pan with white and Madeira wines and boil down to half the volume. Add stock and meat juices. Mix cornstarch with water. Using a wire whisk, gradually stir in cornstarch mixture into sauce. Reduce to desired consistency (cream-like) and adjust seasoning if necessary.

Garnish:
300 g (10 oz) fresh wood mushrooms or 100 g (3 ½ oz) dried (see Method, page 12)
2 Tbsp butter
1 Tbsp finely chopped shallot or onion
1 Tbsp chopped parsley
Salt and pepper, to taste

Clean and slice mushrooms. Sauté in butter with all the remaining ingredients.

Serving suggestion

Place two medallions on the center of each warmed plate, top with a little sauce and garnish with mushrooms. Serve with fettucine or potatoes. (See picture, page 54.)

Substitute

All the deer family, antelope, mountain sheep, lamb and veal medallions.

55

ANTELOPE AND MOUNTAIN SHEEP

ANTELOPE

Antelope yields the leanest and most tender meat of all big game animals and can sometimes be cut without a knife. The meat fibre is very finely grained with a distinctive flavor which can be a real delicacy when served with an appropriate sauce. Virtually all cuts are superb eating and the small legs are ideal when roasted whole.

Ground antelope mixed with pork or other game meats makes delicious meat pies.

The hide can be left on during aging, to minimize drying. Under proper conditions, young animals should be aged for three days, older or rutting animals up to five days.

MOUNTAIN SHEEP

Mountain sheep yields meat which is not as lean as venison. The meat of mature rams is quite coarse but is finer in the female or younger animals. It has a rich but not necessarily gamy flavor which lends itself for use in both venison and lamb recipes.

The hide can be removed before aging. The higher fat content of the mountain sheep will prevent the meat from drying out. Under proper conditions, young mountain sheep should be aged for three days and old animals for up to seven days.

Meat from hind legs yields excellent roasts; the saddle can be roasted whole or cut into racks and chops; shoulder and neck are ideal for stews and ground meat.

Hare Pâté with Apple Salad –
Pages 79, 138
Rack of Mountain Sheep with
Tarragon Sauce, Scalloped
Potatoes – Pages 63, 134
Glazed Blueberries – Page 149

Braised Antelope Shoulder with Onions and Potatoes

Serves 4 to 6

1 shoulder, trimmed, 1 kg (2 lbs)
Salt and pepper, to taste
3 Tbsp olive oil

2 medium onions, sliced
1 clove garlic, crushed
1 tsp thyme
500 mL (2 cups) game stock (see recipe, page 10) or beef broth
4 medium potatoes, peeled and sliced

1 Tbsp chopped fresh chives
(for garnish)

Serving suggestion

Substitute

Preheat oven to 180°C (360°F). Season shoulder with salt and pepper. Heat oil in a large roasting pan over medium high heat. Brown shoulder on all sides. Remove meat and set aside.

Add onions, garlic and thyme to the pan and fry until soft. Return meat to pan and add stock. Cover and place in the oven for 45 minutes. Add the potatoes to the meat and return to the oven. Meat should be tender after a total cooking time of 1½ to 2 hours. Adjust seasoning with salt and pepper.

Slice shoulder against the grain and serve with the onions and potatoes. Sprinkle with chopped chives.

Lamb and mountain sheep shoulder.

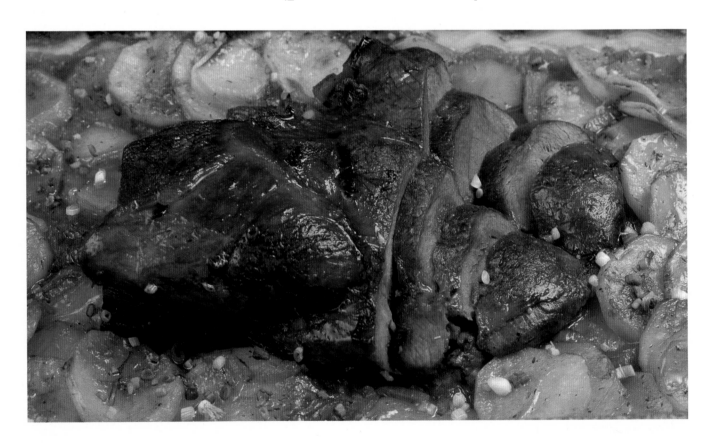

Braised Antelope Shoulder with Onions and Potatoes

58

Antelope in Curry Sauce

Serves 6 to 8

1.5 kg (3 lbs) stewing meat
6 Tbsp olive oil
Salt, to taste

Sauce:
2 large onions, 500 g (1 lb), finely chopped
4 Tbsp curry powder
1 Tbsp ground cumin
2 Tbsp tomato paste
2 bay leaves
250 mL (1 cup) beef broth or water
175 mL (3/4 cup) plain yogurt

Serving suggestion

Substitute

Heat oil in a large heavy bottomed saucepan over medium high heat. Season meat with salt and brown on all sides; do in three batches. Remove meat with a slotted spoon and set aside.

Turn heat down to medium and fry onions until soft, without letting them get brown. Add curry powder, ground cumin, tomato paste and bay leaves and fry for a minute. Deglaze pan with broth. Return meat to the pan and cover tightly. Simmer slowly for 1 1/2 hours or until meat is tender, stirring occasionally. Pour yogurt into a bowl, stir with a wire whisk and add to curry sauce.

Serve with steamed rice (raisins may be added to the rice). A salad on the side will give this meal a nice touch.

Mountain sheep, beef, pork, bear, wild boar, all the deer family and cut up chicken. (When chicken is used, use chicken broth.)

Antelope in Curry Sauce

Antelope Saddle in Cream Sauce

Serves 6

1 saddle, 1.5 kg (3 lbs)
Salt and pepper, to taste
10 juniper berries, crushed
2 Tbsp peanut oil
3 Tbsp butter

Sauce:
150 g (5 oz) trimmings from antelope (optional)
1 medium onion, coarsely chopped
1 medium carrot, coarsely chopped
20 peppercorns
3 cloves
1 cinnamon stick, 20 mm (1 in.) long
1½ Tbsp flour
60 mL (¼ cup) dry white wine
60 mL (¼ cup) Madeira wine
375 mL (1½ cups) whipping cream
1 Tbsp cranberry jelly
Salt and pepper, to taste

Serving suggestion

Substitute

Preheat oven to 230°C (450°F). Rub saddle with salt, pepper and juniper berries. Heat oil and butter in a large heavy bottomed frying or roasting pan over medium high heat. Brown saddle on meat sides and place in the oven, meat side up. Total roasting time will be 35 to 40 minutes.

After 15 minutes, lower oven temperature to 190°C (375°F) and add trimmings (if used), vegetables, peppercorns, cloves and cinnamon stick. Roast for another 20 to 25 minutes, basting occasionally. Remove saddle, set aside on a plate to catch the juices and keep warm.

On the stove, over medium heat, sprinkle flour into pan and fry for 2 minutes. Deglaze pan with white and Madeira wines, scraping off all solids from the bottom of the pan. Stir in cream and cranberry jelly and reduce to desired consistency.

Strain sauce through a fine sieve, pressing trimmings and vegetables with the back of a spoon to get all their juices into the sauce. Adjust seasoning with salt and pepper if necessary.

Carve saddle in front of the guests. Pour a little sauce on warmed plates and arrange meat on top. Complement with young carrots and/or fried mushrooms and green fettucine or any type of roasted potatoes.

Saddle of venison, lamb and mountain sheep.

Mountain Sheep Medallions Glazed with Stilton Sauce

Serves 4

8 medallions from loin or leg, 90 g
(3 oz) each
Salt and pepper, to taste
2 Tbsp peanut oil
2 Tbsp butter

Heat oil and butter in a heavy bottomed frying pan over medium high heat. Season medallions with salt and pepper and fry to your liking. Remove meat, set aside on a plate to catch the juices and keep warm.

Sauce:
125 mL (½ cup) whipping cream
1 tsp cornstarch
1 Tbsp port wine
60 g (2 oz) Stilton or mild blue cheese

Discard frying oil. Pour cream into the pan and boil down to half the volume. Mix cornstarch with port and gradually stir into cream. Add cheese and meat juices; then reduce until sauce becomes very thick.

Spoon sauce over medallions and glaze under the broiler until brown.

Serving suggestion

Place medallions on warmed plates or platter. Serve with spinach and fried potatoes.

Substitute

Lamb medallions and pork chops. (Cook pork chops until well-done.)

Mountain Sheep Roast in Mint Sauce

Serves 4 to 6

1 kg (2 lbs) roast from leg
4 Tbsp olive oil
Salt and pepper, to taste
Thyme, pinch
Rosemary, pinch

Sauce:
1 small onion, coarsely chopped
1 carrot, coarsely chopped
1 stalk celery, coarsely chopped
2 bay leaves
20 peppercorns
4 Tbsp dry white wine
250 mL (1 cup) water
1 Tbsp cornstarch
1 Tbsp cold water
1 Tbsp chopped fresh mint or tarragon
Salt
Lemon juice

Serving suggestion

Substitute

Preheat oven to 200°C (400°F). Heat oil in a large frying or roasting pan over medium high heat. Season roast with salt, pepper, thyme and a little rosemary, and brown on all sides. Place in the oven and roast for 20 minutes.

Add vegetables, bay leaves and peppercorns. Lower oven temperature to 190°C (375°F) and roast for 30 minutes more. Baste roast once or twice. Remove meat, set aside on a plate to catch the juices and keep warm.

Deglaze pan with wine and water. Bring liquid to a boil and simmer for 5 minutes. Strain liquid and vegetables through a sieve, pressing the vegetables to get all their juices into the sauce and stir. Mix cornstarch with water. Using a wire whisk, gradually stir in cornstarch mixture to thicken sauce. Add meat juices and mint to sauce and adjust seasoning with salt and a touch of lemon juice.

Carve roast into thin slices, arrange on warmed plates or platter and pour sauce over. Serve with scalloped potatoes (see recipe, page 134) and green beans.

Domestic lamb and antelope.

Rack of Mountain Sheep with Tarragon Sauce

Serves 4

4 racks, trimmed, 250 g (9 oz) each
Salt and pepper, to taste
Thyme, pinch
Rosemary, pinch
4 Tbsp olive oil

Preheat oven to 230°C (450°F). Season racks with salt, pepper, thyme and a little rosemary. Heat oil in a heavy bottomed roasting pan over medium high heat. Place racks, meat side down, into pan and put in the oven for 15 minutes.

Sauce:
1 small onion, coarsely chopped
1/2 small carrot, coarsely chopped
1 stalk celery, coarsely chopped
2 bay leaves
15 peppercorns, crushed
1 clove garlic
4 Tbsp dry white wine
250 mL (1 cup) broth or water
2 tsp tarragon
2 Tbsp port wine

Lower oven temperature to 190°C (375°F), turn meat over; add all vegetables, bay leaves, peppercorns and garlic. Roast for 15 more minutes basting meat once or twice. Total cooking time should be around 30 minutes for medium. Remove meat, set aside on a plate to catch the juices and keep warm.

Discard most of the frying oil and set pan on the stove. Deglaze pan with wine and broth and boil down to half the volume. Strain liquid and vegetables through a fine wire sieve. Stir in meat juices, tarragon and port; bring to a boil and serve or keep warm. (Sauce may be thickened with a little cornstarch, if desired.)

Serving suggestion

Cut racks into chops, pour sauce on warmed plates and place meat on top. Serve with scalloped potatoes (see recipe, page 134) and either fried zucchini with tomatoes or green beans.

Substitute

Rack of venison, domestic lamb and antelope.

BEAR AND WILD BOAR

Although bear and wild boar are not related, their meats and textures are very close to that of pork but much darker. The meat from young animals is tender and delicately flavored, and can be used for delicious roasts and chops. Meat from adult animals should be marinated and meat from old animals should be avoided.

Remove skin of bear and boar before aging, the large amount of fat will prevent meat from drying out. In proper conditions, age young animals for three days and adult animals for five days. All fat should be trimmed off the meat when butchering.

Trichinea is a small parasite which causes trichinosis; it may be found in the meat of bears, wild boar and domestic pigs. To kill this organism, always cook these meats to an internal temperature of 58°C (136°F), which is well done, not pink. Or freeze the meat at -15°C (0°F) for twenty days if pieces are less than 15 cm (6 in.) thick. Freeze thicker pieces for thirty days.

Bear Loin Marinated in Vinegar and Raspberries

Serves 6

1.5 kg (3 lbs) loin

Marinade:
2 Tbsp oil
1 small onion, coarsely chopped
1 clove garlic, crushed
1 small carrot, coarsely chopped
125 mL (½ cup) red wine vinegar
250 mL (1 cup) water
125 mL (½ cup) raspberries, fresh or frozen
2 Tbsp honey
30 peppercorns
1 tsp thyme
1 bay leaf
3 cloves
Salt and pepper, to taste

2 Tbsp oil

1 Tbsp cornstarch
1 Tbsp cold water
Pepper, freshly ground

Serving suggestion

Substitute

Trim loin of all fat. Wash in cold water and set aside.

Heat oil in a frying pan over medium heat. Fry onion, garlic and carrot until soft; stir in vinegar and boil down until just dry. Add water, raspberries, honey and all herbs, then bring to a boil. Remove the pan from heat and let cool.

Rub meat with salt and pepper and place in a glass or earthenware dish (not metal). Pour cool marinade on top and cover with plastic wrap or cloth. Place in the refrigerator and marinate overnight, turning meat once.

Preheat oven to 190°C (375°F). Remove loin from marinade and dry with a paper towel. Heat oil in a frying or roasting pan over medium high heat. Brown meat on all sides. Pour marinade over the meat, cover and place in the oven. Braise for 1 hour or until meat is tender. Remove meat, set aside and keep warm.

Strain liquid and vegetables through a fine sieve. There should be 250 mL (1 cup) liquid; otherwise, add water or boil down. Mix cornstarch with water. Bring liquid to a boil; then gradually stir in cornstarch mixture to thicken sauce. Adjust seasoning with freshly ground pepper.

Cut loin into slices, arrange on warmed plates or platter and pour sauce on top. Complement with rice or potatoes and brussel sprouts or broccoli. Garnish with fresh raspberries, if available.

Loin, leg and shoulder roast from wild boar, pork, and bear. (When using leg or shoulder roast, braise longer.)

Bear Stew
Serves 6

1.5 kg (3 lbs) stewing meat
4 Tbsp lard or peanut oil
Salt and pepper, to taste

Remove all fat and cut stewing meat into bite-sized pieces. Heat lard in a heavy bottomed saucepan over medium high heat. Season meat with salt and pepper and brown on all sides. (Do one-third the quantity at a time.) Remove meat with a slotted spoon and set aside.

1 small onion, chopped
1 clove garlic, chopped
1 Tbsp tomato paste
4 Tbsp flour
1 Tbsp red wine vinegar
125 mL (1/2 cup) dry red wine
375 mL (1 1/2 cups) beef broth
1/2 tsp thyme
1/2 tsp ground cinnamon
2 bay leaves
10 juniper berries

When all meat has been browned and removed, turn heat down to medium. Fry onion and garlic until lightly brown. Add tomato paste and flour, and fry for a few more minutes. Stir in vinegar and wine, scraping off all solids from bottom of pan. Add broth and bring to a boil, stirring constantly. Return meat to the pan, add all herbs and juniper berries; cover and simmer slowly for 2 hours or until the meat is tender. Stir occasionally and add water if sauce becomes too thick.

Garnish:
6 Tbsp cranberry sauce
100 g (3 1/2 oz) toasted almond flakes

(See Serving suggestion.)

Serving suggestion

Place stew on warm plates or in a deep serving dish and garnish with cranberry sauce and almonds. Serve with boiled potatoes, fried briefly in butter. Complement with a salad on the side.

Substitute

Wild boar, all the deer family, mountain sheep and antelope.

Casserole of Wild Boar Chops with Rice

Serves 4

8 chops 100 g (3½ oz) each
Salt and pepper, to taste
1 Tbsp Dijon mustard
4 Tbsp oil
Flour

2 small onions, sliced
1 clove garlic, crushed

250 mL (1 cup) rice
796 mL (28 fl oz) peeled tomatoes,
fresh or canned
1 tsp thyme
2 bay leaves

Serving suggestion

Substitute

Preheat oven to 180°C (360°F). Trim meat of all fat and skin. Season with salt and pepper, then brush with mustard. Heat oil in a casserole or saucepan over medium high heat. Dip meat into flour and shake off excess. Brown on both sides. Remove meat and set aside.

Turn heat down to medium; sauté onions and garlic until soft but not brown. Remove and set aside.

Arrange casserole in layers, starting with half the quantity of: rice, chops, onion, tomatoes and herbs; repeat in the same order. Cover and place in the oven for 1¼ hours.

Serve in casserole dish and complement with a salad on the side.

Bear and pork chops.

Casserole of Wild Boar Chops with Rice

Marinated Wild Boar Roast

Serves 4

1 kg (2 lbs) roast from loin or leg

Marinade:
30 juniper berries, crushed
30 black peppercorns, crushed
2 Tbsp gin

Salt, to taste
2 Tbsp oil
1 small onion, coarsely chopped
125 mL (1/2 cup) water

Sprinkle roast with juniper berries and peppercorns; place in a bowl. Pour gin over meat, cover with plastic wrap and marinate overnight in the refrigerator.

Preheat oven to 200°C (400°F). Season meat with salt and place with oil into a roasting pan. Put in the oven and roast until brown, about 20 minutes. Lower oven temperature to 190°C (375°F), add onion and roast for 10 more minutes. Pour water over meat and roast for 1 hour or until meat is tender; baste occasionally. (If the top of the roast gets too brown, cover with aluminum foil.) Remove roast and strain the juices through a fine sieve.

Serving suggestion

Slice roast, and arrange on warmed plates or platter. Serve meat juices on the side and complement with mashed potatoes and brussel sprouts or red cabbage (see recipe, page 135).

Substitute

Bear and pork.

RABBIT AND HARE

These small game animals offer great eating. The dark meat of jack rabbits (large hares), has more flavor than the light meat of rabbits and snowshoe hares. Young animals are the most tender, and best used for roasting and frying. The meat of older animals is drier and tougher and therefore best used for braising and stewing. Either can be used for flavorful meat pies and pâtés. The saddle is the choicest cut. The kidneys, fried, are a delicacy. Many chicken recipes work very well with rabbit as the taste and some of the cuts are similar.

Young animals can be distinguished from old ones since on the young the skin and bones break easily.

Rabbit and hare should be skinned and aged in the refrigerator for three days before cooking.

Spinach Soup with Croutons —
Page 13
Wild Duck Casserole — Page 108
Apricot Dumplings — Page 153

Rabbit Casserole

Serves 4

1 young rabbit
Salt and pepper, to taste
Flour
4 Tbsp olive oil

Preheat oven to 190°C (375°F). Cut rabbit into pieces (see Butchering). Season meat with salt and pepper. Dip into flour and shake off excess. Heat 3 Tbsp of the oil in a frying pan over medium high heat. Brown meat on all sides. Remove meat and place in an ovenproof casserole.

1 small onion, sliced
2 cloves garlic, finely chopped
100 g (3½ oz) mushrooms, sliced
1 green bell pepper, sliced
540 mL (19 fl oz) peeled tomatoes, fresh or canned
½ tsp thyme
⅓ tsp basil
2 bay leaves

Turn heat down to medium and add remaining oil to the pan. Fry onion, garlic, mushrooms and green pepper for about 5 minutes. Add tomatoes and herbs, bring to a boil and pour over rabbit pieces. Cover, place in the oven and bake for approximately 1¼ hours or until meat is tender.

If thicker sauce is desired, remove rabbit, place sauce back on the stove and reduce to desired consistency.

Serving suggestion

Serve in the casserole and complement with steamed rice.

Substitute

2 chickens.

Breaded Rabbit with Herbs

Serves 4

1 rabbit plus liver
Salt and pepper, to taste
Flour
2 eggs, beaten
250 mL (1 cup) breadcrumbs
1 Tbsp chopped parsley
1 tsp basil

Preheat oven to 175°C (350°F). Cut rabbit into pieces and trim liver (see Butchering). Season with salt and pepper. Have three bowls: one with flour, one with the eggs and one with a mixture of breadcrumbs, parsley and basil. First dip meat into flour and shake off excess. Second, dip into the eggs. Third, coat with breadcrumbs mixture.

5 Tbsp butter

Lemon, cut into wedges (for garnish)

Heat butter in a large frying pan over medium heat. Brown meat pieces on one side, turn them and place in the oven. Roast for about 25 to 30 minutes, basting meat once halfway through cooking time.

Serving suggestion

Arrange on a warmed platter and garnish with lemon wedges. Complement with rice or parsley potatoes and a salad on the side.

Substitute

Skinned chicken pieces, pork, veal chops, game fowl and poultry liver. (For liver, cut cooking time in half.)

Braised Rabbit in Tarragon Sauce

Serves 3 to 4

1 rabbit 1.5 kg (3 lbs)
Salt and pepper, to taste
1 Tbsp peanut oil
2 Tbsp butter

Preheat oven to 180°C (360°F). Wash rabbit in cold water and dry with a paper towel. Cut rabbit into pieces (see Butchering) and season with salt and pepper. Heat oil and butter in a large saucepan over medium high heat. Brown meat on all sides, remove and set aside.

Sauce:
2 Tbsp flour
125 mL (1/2 cup) dry white wine
250 mL (1 cup) chicken broth
125 mL (1/2 cup) whipping cream
2 tsp chopped tarragon, fresh or 1 tsp dried
Salt and pepper, to taste

Turn heat down to medium. Using the same pan, add flour and stir. Deglaze pan with wine and broth, bring to a boil, stirring constantly with a wire whisk. Return meat to the pan, cover and place in the oven for 1 to 1 1/2 hours or until meat is tender. Place pan back on the stove, remove meat, set aside on a serving dish and keep warm. If there is any fat on top of the sauce, skim off with a spoon. Stir in cream, add tarragon and bring to a boil. Adjust seasoning with salt and pepper. Pour sauce over rabbit.

Serving suggestion

Serve with rice mixed with sweet corn kernels or peas.

Substitute

Chicken (remove skin and any fat).

Rabbit Legs in Green Peppercorn Sauce

Serves 4

2 rabbits are needed for this recipe.

4 hind legs of rabbit (see Butchering)
Salt and pepper, to taste
Flour
2 Tbsp oil
2 Tbsp butter

Preheat oven to 190°C (375°F). Season meat with salt and pepper, dip into flour and shake off excess. Heat oil and butter in a frying pan over medium high heat. Brown legs lightly on one side, turn them and place in the oven. Roast for about 30 minutes or until done, basting occasionally. Remove meat, set aside and keep warm.

Sauce:
1 Tbsp chopped shallots or onion
1 Tbsp green peppercorns
4 Tbsp dry white wine
2 Tbsp brandy
125 mL (1/2 cup) game stock (see recipe, page 10) or chicken broth
250 mL (1 cup) whipping cream
1 Tbsp Dijon mustard
Salt, to taste

Discard frying oil, leaving 1 Tbsp. Over medium high heat, sauté shallots and green peppercorns briefly. Deglaze pan with wine and brandy and boil down liquid to half the volume. Pour in the stock and cream; reduce to a creamy consistency. Stir in mustard and adjust seasoning with salt if necessary.

Serving suggestion

Place meat on warmed plates and pour sauce over. Complement with fettuccine and glazed carrots or any colorful vegetable.

Substitute

Whole rabbit and chicken, cut into pieces (see Butchering).

Rabbit Legs in Green Peppercorn Sauce

74

Hare Loins Wrapped in Bacon with Sour Cream Sauce

Serves 2 to 4

2 loins from hare (see Butchering)
Salt and pepper, to taste
4 slices bacon
2 Tbsp oil

Preheat oven to 230°C (450°F). Season meat with salt and pepper. Wrap with bacon and secure with toothpicks. Heat oil in a large frying pan over medium high heat. Quickly brown meat on all sides; then place in the oven for 5 to 7 minutes. Remove meat, set aside on a plate to catch the juices and wrap in foil to keep warm.

Sauce:
1 Tbsp chopped shallots or onion
125 mL (¹/₂ cup) sour cream
Salt and pepper, to taste

3 green onions, chopped (for garnish)

Discard frying oil, leaving 1 Tbsp. Sauté shallots briefly and stir in the sour cream. Bring to a boil and adjust seasoning with salt and pepper. Add meat juices to the sauce and stir.

Serving suggestion

Slice fillets on an angle and arrange on warmed plates. Pour sauce over and sprinkle with green onions. Serve with mashed potatoes and a salad on the side.

Braised Legs of Hare in Pepper Sauce

Serves 4

2 hares are needed for this recipe.

4 hind legs of hare (see Butchering)
100 g (3¹/₂ oz) pork back fat
(approximately)
2 Tbsp peanut oil
2 Tbsp butter
Salt and pepper, to taste
10 juniper berries, crushed

Sauce:
1 small onion, coarsely chopped
1 small carrot, coarsely chopped
¹/₂ Tbsp tomato paste
2 Tbsp flour
40 peppercorns, crushed
¹/₂ tsp thyme
2 bay leaves
250 mL (1 cup) game stock (see recipe,
page 10) or chicken broth
125 mL (¹/₂ cup) whipping cream
1 Tbsp Dijon mustard
Pepper, freshly ground

Serving suggestion

Substitute

Preheat oven to 180°C (360°F). Lard legs with pork fat. (This will prevent meat from becoming too dry.) Heat oil and butter in a frying or roasting pan over medium high heat. Season meat with salt, pepper and juniper berries. Brown on all sides. Remove meat and set aside.

Turn heat down to medium. In the same pan, add onion and carrot and fry until onion is soft. Add tomato paste, flour, peppercorns and herbs and fry for a few minutes more. Pour in the stock, scraping off all solids from the bottom. Bring to a boil. Return meat to the pan, cover and place in the oven. Braise for 1 to 2 hours or until meat is tender. Remove meat, set aside and keep warm. Strain sauce through a sieve, pressing the vegetables to get all their juices into the sauce. Stir in cream and bring to a boil. Adjust seasoning with mustard and freshly ground pepper.

Arrange meat on warmed plates or platter and pour sauce over. Serve with fettuccine, spaetzle (see recipe, page 137) or roesti (see recipe, page 134) and carrots or fried mushrooms.

Any piece of hare, rabbit, wild goose and duck. (Remove skin of goose and duck.)

Saddle of Hare in Cream Sauce with Gin

Serves 4 to 6

2 hares are needed for this recipe.

2 saddles of hare (see Butchering)
Salt and pepper, to taste
20 juniper berries, crushed
2 Tbsp olive oil
2 Tbsp butter

Preheat oven to 200°C (400°F). Season saddles with salt and pepper and rub with juniper berries. Heat oil and butter in a heavy bottomed frying pan over medium high heat. Brown saddles on meat sides and place in the oven, meat side up. Roast for 10 minutes, basting once. Remove meat, set aside on a plate to catch the juices and keep warm.

Sauce:
1 shallot or 1 Tbsp onion, finely chopped
4 Tbsp gin
175 mL (³/₄ cup) whipping cream
125 mL (¹/₂ cup) game stock (see recipe, page 10) or chicken broth
Salt, to taste
Pepper, freshly ground

Discard frying oil, leaving 1 Tbsp. Turn heat down to medium, add shallot and sauté briefly. Deglaze pan with gin and boil down liquid to half the volume. Pour in cream and stock; reduce sauce to a creamy consistency. Add meat juices and adjust seasoning with salt and freshly ground pepper. Pour sauce over meat and place back in the oven for 2 to 3 minutes to reheat.

Serving suggestion

Carve saddle, pour a little sauce on warmed plates and arrange meat on top. Serve with fried mushrooms and spaetzle (see recipe, page 137).

Substitute

Rabbit.

Hasenpfeffer (Jugged Hare)

Serves 4 to 6

1 hare

Cut hare into pieces (see Butchering). Wash in cold water and dry with a paper towel.

Marinade:
375 mL (1½ cups) heavy dry red wine
2 Tbsp red wine vinegar
3 Tbsp brandy
2 bay leaves
1 tsp thyme
1 cinnamon stick 20 mm (1 in.)
30 peppercorns, crushed
10 juniper berries, crushed

Combine all ingredients for marinade in a glass or plastic bowl (not metal). Add meat to marinade and set in the refrigerator for 2 hours. Remove meat and dry with a paper towel. (Set marinade aside for later use.)

5 slices bacon, cut into strips
Salt and pepper, to taste

In a large saucepan, fry bacon over medium heat. When bacon is crisp, remove with a slotted spoon and set aside. Season meat with salt and pepper and brown on all sides in the bacon fat. Remove meat and set aside.

1 shallot, finely chopped
3 Tbsp flour
300 mL (1¼ cups) beef broth
2 Tbsp cranberry jelly
Salt and pepper, to taste

In the same pan, sauté shallot briefly, add flour and fry for a minute or two. (Add butter if fat is insufficient.) Deglaze pan with marinade, scraping off all solids from the bottom. Bring to a boil and pour in the broth. Return meat to the sauce and cover. Cook slowly for 1 to 2 hours or until meat is tender. Remove meat and place in a serving dish. Stir cranberry jelly into sauce and adjust seasoning with salt and pepper. Strain sauce over hare and sprinkle with reserved bacon.

Serving suggestion

Serve with servietten knoedel (see recipe, page 138) or spaetzle (see recipe, page 137) and red cabbage (see recipe, page 135) or carrots.

78

Hare Pâté (Jack Rabbit)

1 hare is needed for this recipe.

400 g (14 oz) hare meat from hind legs,
trimmed
200 g (7 oz) lean pork
200 g (7 oz) pork back fat
1 hare liver or 100 g (3½ oz) chicken
livers, trimmed
2 Tbsp butter
1 shallot, sliced or 1 Tbsp chopped
onion
1 clove garlic, crushed

Marinade:
1 Tbsp salt
30 peppercorns, crushed
½ tsp nutmeg
1 tsp tarragon
½ tsp thyme
1 bay leaf
10 juniper berries
2 Tbsp brandy
1 Tbsp port wine

Pâté dough:
500 g (3½ cups) flour
250 g (9 oz) butter
1 tsp salt
2 eggs
60 mL (¼ cup) water (approximately)

Garnish:
2 Tbsp butter
2 loins from hare (see Butchering)
Salt and pepper, to taste
200 g (7 oz) mushrooms, sliced

1 slice white bread
1 Tbsp milk
1 egg
250 mL (1 cup) whipping cream

Preparing the ingredients:
Cut all meats into large cubes. Heat butter in a large frying pan over medium high heat. Sauté hare meat, liver, shallot and garlic for about 30 seconds (meat and liver should stay rare inside). Remove these ingredients, place in a glass or plastic bowl (not metal) and mix in pork.

Add all ingredients of the marinade to the meat and mix thoroughly. Cover with plastic wrap, place in refrigerator and marinate overnight. Before processing, place marinated meat into the freezer for 30 minutes. (This will prevent meat from overheating during processing.)

Prepare pâté dough as pie dough on page 120.

Prepare garnish:
Heat butter in a frying pan over medium heat. Season loins with salt and pepper and brown briefly on all sides (loins should stay rare inside). Remove meat and place in refrigerator to cool. In the same pan, fry mushrooms. Remove and place in refrigerator to cool.

Processing:
Soak bread with milk. Remove marinated meat from freezer and mix in bread and egg. Blend in a food processor (do half the mixture at a time), adding cream while blending. Process only long enough to get a smooth texture (forcemeat should stay cool). Remove and place in refrigerator.

Butter (to grease mold)

Egg wash: 1 egg yolk beaten with
1 Tbsp milk

Aspic:
1½ Tbsp unflavored gelatin
4 Tbsp port wine
500 mL (2 cups) clear chicken broth

Serving suggestion

Substitute

Assembling the pâté: (See picture, page 81.)

Preheat oven to 230°C (450°F). On a floured surface, roll out dough to a 3 mm (1/8 in.) thickness. (Remember to set aside sufficient dough to cover mold.) Butter a 33 cm x 12 cm x 6 cm (13 in. x 5 in. x 2½ in.) mold and line with the dough, leaving 10 mm (½ in.) overhang.

Stir mushrooms into forcemeat. Spread 20 mm (1 in.) layer of forcemeat over the bottom of the mold. Place hare loins on top along the length and cover with remaining forcemeat. Fold edges of the dough over the top and brush with egg wash. Cover with dough, trim edges and press down around the edges with the back of a fork. Cut 2 small holes in the dough (to allow steam to escape) and put a cylinder of foil in each hole. Brush with egg wash and place in the oven. After 15 minutes, lower oven temperature to 180°C (360°F) and bake for another 50 minutes. Remove and let cool for 8 hours or overnight at room temperature.

Finishing the pâté:

Sprinkle gelatin on port; let stand for 1 minute. Bring broth to a boil and add to wine, stir until gelatine is dissolved. When aspic is cold but not set, fill pâté through one of the steam holes. Place in the refrigerator to set. (If there is leftover aspic, let set, chop and serve with pâté.) Pâté will keep for 1 week in the refrigerator or it can be frozen.

Serve with apple salad (see recipe, page 138) or pickled vegetables such as onions and beets.

All game meat (except moose, bear and boar) with their natural flavor are ideal for making pâtés or terrines. For the best results, use only best quality meat; otherwise, much effort may be wasted.

Note: If a food processor is not available, grind forcemeat twice through the finest blade of a meat grinder.

If dough crust leaks when filling pâté with aspic, seal with soft butter. Remove butter after aspic has set.

If pâté is difficult to unmold, place mold in warm water for 1 minute.

For a more colorful look, add 150 g (5 oz) diced cooked ham and/or 100 g (3½ oz) whole pistachio nuts to forcemeat.

Terrine: This recipe can also be used for a terrine. Line the terrine form with thin sheets of pork fat, fill with forcemeat as above. Cover with pork fat and place in a water bath. Bake in 180°C (360°F) for 60 to 70 minutes. Serve as above and/or with toast.

Assembling the pâté:

Line mold with the dough.

Brush with egg wash.

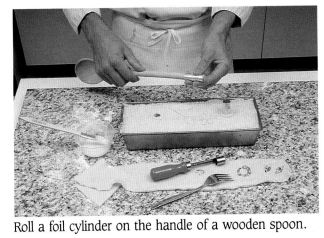
Roll a foil cylinder on the handle of a wooden spoon.

Fill pâté with cold aspic.

Pâté or Terrine.

UPLAND BIRDS AND WATERFOWL

For information about the handling of game birds, see page 174.

Quail Breasts and Chicken Liver on Salad

Serves 6 as an appetizer or 4 as a light lunch

1 Belgian endive
1 butter lettuce
¹/₂ bunch spinach
9 cherry tomatoes
30 seedless grapes, cut in half

6 chicken livers
4 Tbsp olive oil
6 quails, (12 breasts) skin removed and deboned (see Butchering)
Salt and pepper, to taste

Dressing:
1 Tbsp chopped shallots
2 Tbsp sherry vinegar
1 Tbsp port wine
2 Tbsp olive oil
Salt and pepper, to taste

Serving suggestion

Substitute

Core Belgian endive and cut into 10 mm (¹/₂ in.) pieces. Tear butter lettuce and spinach into bite-sized pieces. Wash, drain and mix all greens together. Divide onto dinner plates. Garnish salads with cherry tomatoes and grapes.

Trim and cut livers into 3 pieces each. Heat oil in a large heavy bottomed frying pan over medium heat. Season quail breasts with salt and pepper and sauté until nearly done (breasts should be kept a little pink inside). Remove meat, set aside on a plate to catch the juices and keep warm. Repeat with chicken livers.

Add shallots to the frying pan and sauté briefly. Stir in vinegar, port and oil, scraping off all solids from the bottom of the pan. Add meat juices, bring just to a boil and season with salt and pepper.

Arrange quail breasts and chicken livers on salads and pour over hot dressing. Serve immediately.

Use any lettuce in season, except head lettuce. If sherry vinegar is not available, use a good wine vinegar.

Note: Use quail carcasses to prepare stock (see recipe, page 10).

Roast Quails with Grape Sauce

Serves 4

8 quails
2 Tbsp butter
Salt and pepper, to taste

Sauce:
125 mL (½ cup) chicken broth
1 tsp cornstarch
60 mL (¼ cup) Madeira wine
40 seedless green grapes, cut in half
Pepper, freshly ground

Serving suggestion

Preheat oven to 230°C (450°F). Heat butter in a large frying pan over medium heat. Rub birds with salt and pepper. Brown quails on all sides. Place in the oven for 15 minutes. Remove birds, set aside on a plate to catch the juices and keep warm.

Discard frying butter and place pan back on the stove. Pour in broth and bring to a boil. Mix cornstarch with Madeira. Using a wire whisk, gradually stir cornstarch mixture into the boiling broth. Add grapes and meat juices to the sauce. Adjust seasoning with freshly ground pepper.

Place 2 quails on each warmed plate and pour sauce over. Serve with rice (half wild) mixed with toasted flaked almonds. Complement with a salad on the side.

Note: Do not be afraid to eat quail using fingers, even in a restaurant.

Roast Quails with Grape Sauce

Stuffed Quails in Sherry Sauce

Serves 6

12 quails

Stuffing:
250 g (9 oz) chicken breast, skin removed
2 chicken livers, trimmed
2 Tbsp butter
1 shallot, chopped
100 g (3½ oz) mushrooms, sliced
2 Tbsp port wine
½ tsp salt
Pepper, pinch
1 slice white bread soaked with 1 Tbsp cream
60 mL (¼ cup) whipping cream
Butter

Sauce:
60 mL (¼ cup) sherry wine
125 mL (½ cup) whipping cream
375 mL (1½ cups) basic game bird sauce (see recipe, page 11)
Salt and pepper, to taste
30 green seedless grapes, cut in half

Serving suggestion

Debone birds from the back (see Butchering).

Heat butter in a frying pan over medium heat. Sauté liver briefly on both sides, remove and set aside. (Liver should still be rare in the middle.) In the same pan, add shallot and mushrooms and fry for a few minutes. Pour in port and boil down until just dry. Set aside and let cool completely.

When cool, place all stuffing ingredients, except cream, into a food processor. Process for a minute, adding the cream slowly. (If a food processor is not available, pass meat twice through the finest blade of a grinder. Place bowl over ice water and stir in cream.)

Preheat oven to 230°C (450°F). Place stuffing on the middle of the birds and fold meat over. Set quails on a buttered roasting pan (see Note) and brush with softened butter. Season with salt and pepper. Roast in the oven for 20 minutes. Remove and set aside.

Deglaze pan with sherry, cream and basic sauce; reduce to a creamy consistency. Adjust seasoning with salt and pepper, then add grapes to the sauce.

Cut quails in half and arrange on warm plates. Pour sauce on top and serve with broccoli and fried potato rolls (see recipe, page 139) or fried potatoes.

Note: Since quails are not sewn together, choose one of the following methods to prevent them from opening while cooking: Place birds, breast side up, closely together in a pan; hold together with a thin slice of bacon tied with kitchen string; place bird on a square of buttered foil which is then folded up around the sides of the bird. (See picture, page 187.)

Grouse in Casserole

Serves 4

2 grouse
3 Tbsp butter
Salt and pepper, to taste

150 g (5 oz) mushrooms, cut into quarters
200 g (7 oz) pearl pickling onions, fresh or frozen
1 small onion, chopped
1 clove garlic
1 small carrot, chopped
20 peppercorns, crushed
Thyme, pinch
Rosemary, pinch
1 bay leaf
2 Tbsp flour
2 Tbsp brandy
60 mL (¼ cup) dry red wine
250 mL (1 cup) game bird stock (see recipe, page 10) or chicken broth

Serving suggestion

Substitute

Preheat oven to 180°C (360°F). Cut birds in half. Heat butter in a frying pan over medium heat. Season grouse with salt and pepper and brown on both sides. Remove birds and place into an ovenproof casserole.

Add mushrooms and pearl onions to the pan and sauté briefly. Transfer with a slotted spoon into casserole. In the same pan, add chopped onion, garlic and carrot and fry until onion is soft. Add all herbs and flour; fry for a further minute. Stir in brandy and wine, scraping off solids from the bottom of the pan. Boil down liquid to half the volume. Add stock and simmer for 20 minutes. (If sauce is too thick, add a little water.)

Strain sauce through a sieve over the grouse, pressing vegetables to get all their juices into the sauce. Cover and place in the oven for 50 to 60 minutes.

Serve with parsley potatoes.

4 partridges, 2 pheasants or 1 rabbit.

Braised Grouse

Serves 4

3 or 4 grouse (older birds can be used)
2 Tbsp oil
2 Tbsp butter
Salt and pepper, to taste
Thyme, pinch
Flour

½ small onion, finely chopped
1 small carrot, finely chopped
100 g (3½ oz) mushrooms, finely chopped
2 Tbsp flour
60 mL (¼ cup) dry white wine
375 mL (1½ cups) game bird stock (see recipe, page 10) or chicken broth

60 mL (¼ cup) whipping cream
2 Tbsp cranberry jelly

Serving suggestion

Substitute

Preheat oven to 180°C (360°F). Remove skin and cut birds in quarters (see Butchering). Wash birds with cold water and pat dry with a paper towel. Heat oil and butter in a large saucepan over medium heat. Season grouse with salt, pepper and thyme, dip into flour and shake off excess. Brown on both sides. Remove meat and set aside.

Add onion, carrot and mushrooms to pan and fry until onion is soft. Stir in flour and fry for a minute. Deglaze pan with wine, scraping off solids from the bottom of the pan. Add stock and bring to a boil. Return meat to the pan, cover and put in the oven for 1 to 1½ hours or until meat is tender. Remove meat, place in a serving dish and keep warm.

On the stove bring sauce to a boil and stir in the cream and cranberry jelly. Reduce to a creamy consistency and adjust seasoning if necessary. Pour sauce over meat.

Serve with snow peas and roesti (see recipe, page 134) or spaetzle (see recipe, page 137).

2 pheasants or 4 partridges.

Roast Grouse with Juniper Berries and Cream Sauce

Serves 4

2 grouse
2 Tbsp butter
Salt and pepper, to taste
1 tsp juniper berries, finely crushed

Preheat oven to 230°C (450°F). Tie birds (see Butchering). Melt butter in a frying or roasting pan over medium heat. Rub grouse with salt, pepper and juniper berries. Brush with melted butter, place on their sides in the pan and put in the oven.

Roasting time will be 30 minutes. Roast 10 minutes on each side, then turn birds breast side up for the last 10 minutes. Baste at each turn with frying butter. Remove birds, set aside and keep warm.

Sauce:
2 Tbsp gin
375 mL (1½ cups) whipping cream
1 Tbsp cranberry jelly
Salt and pepper, to taste

Discard frying butter and place pan over medium high heat. Deglaze pan with gin and boil down liquid to half the volume. Stir in cream, scraping off solids from the bottom of the pan. Bring to a boil and reduce to a creamy consistency. Add cranberry jelly and adjust seasoning with salt and pepper.

Serving suggestion

Cut grouse in half, arrange on warmed plates and pour sauce over. Serve with fried potatoes and asparagus.

Substitute

4 partridges or 2 pheasants. (Total cooking time for pheasant is 35 to 40 minutes.)

Roast Grouse with Juniper Berries and Cream Sauce

Stuffed Partridge with Cream Sauce

Serves 4 to 6

4 partridges

Wash cavities with cold water and drain.

Stuffing:
1 egg
1 Tbsp whipping cream
4 slices white bread, cubed
1 Tbsp butter
1 small onion, chopped
2 slices bacon, cut into strips
100 g (3½ oz) mushrooms, sliced

Beat egg and cream together and pour over bread. Heat butter in a frying pan and fry onion, bacon and mushrooms until soft. Place in a bowl and mix in all the other stuffing ingredients. Fill cavities with stuffing and tie birds (see Butchering).

4 Tbsp butter
Salt and pepper, to taste

Preheat oven to 190°C (375°F). Heat butter in a large frying pan over medium heat. Rub partridges with salt and pepper. Brush birds with melted butter, place on their sides in the pan and put in the oven. Roasting time will be 45 minutes. Roast 20 minutes on each side, then turn birds breast side up for the last 5 minutes. Baste at each turn. Remove birds, set aside and keep warm.

Sauce:
125 mL (½ cup) dry white wine
250 mL (1 cup) whipping cream
Salt and pepper, to taste

Discard frying butter and place pan back on the stove. Deglaze pan with wine and boil down liquid to one-fourth of the volume. Add cream and reduce to a creamy consistency. (Do not reduce too much; otherwise, sauce will curdle.) Adjust seasoning with salt and pepper.

Serving suggestion

Pour sauce on warmed plates, cut birds in half and place on top. Serve with green peas and carrots.

Substitute

Grouse.

90

Roast Partridge with Bacon

Serves 4

4 partridges
Salt and pepper, to taste
8 slices bacon

Preheat oven to 230°C (450°F). Rub birds with a little salt and pepper. Tie 2 slices of bacon over the breast of each bird with kitchen string.

2 Tbsp butter

Melt butter in a frying or roasting pan over medium high heat. Put birds into pan and roast for 15 minutes in the oven. Remove pan from the oven, cut strings and place bacon on the bottom of the pan. Put birds over bacon, baste and place back in the oven for 10 minutes to brown the breasts. Remove meat and set aside in a warm place for 10 minutes before carving.

Serving suggestion

Cut partridges in half and place with bacon on warmed plates. Serve with creamed brussel sprouts and parsley potatoes.

Substitute

Grouse (prolong cooking time by 5 minutes).

Note: For variety, roast partridges without bacon. Serve with apple sauce or bread sauce (see recipe, page 98) with cranberry sauce on the side. Complement with scalloped potatoes (see recipe, page 134).

Braised Partridge in Cabbage Leaves

Serves 4 to 6

4 partridges (older birds can be used)
3 Tbsp butter
Salt and pepper, to taste

Remove skin and cut partridges in half. Heat butter in a frying pan over medium heat. Season birds with salt and pepper. Brown on both sides. Remove birds and set aside.

1 medium cabbage
2 slices bacon, cut into strips
Marjoram, pinch

Preheat oven to 190°C (375°F). Prepare cabbage as shown on page 119. Reserve 8 larger leaves and cut remaining leaves into fine strips. In the same pan, over medium heat, fry bacon and cabbage strips for a few minutes. Season with salt, pepper and marjoram, then remove from heat. Divide on top of the partridge halves and wrap halves in the reserved cabbage leaves.

1 Tbsp butter
1 small onion, chopped
250 mL (1 cup) whipping cream

Grease a large roasting pan with butter and sprinkle the bottom with the onion. Arrange partridges side by side, cabbage ends down, over onion. Place in the oven and roast for 15 minutes. Pour cream over the birds, cover and braise for approximately 50 minutes or until birds are tender. Sauce should now have the right consistency (cream-like); otherwise, remove birds and reduce to desired consistency.

Serving suggestion

Place birds on warmed plates or platter and pour sauce on top. Serve with boiled potatoes.

Substitute

Grouse.

Braised Partridge in Cabbage Leaves

Pheasant Breasts with Wood Mushrooms

Serves 6

3 pheasants, (6 breasts)
(see Butchering)
2 Tbsp butter
Salt and pepper, to taste

Preheat oven to 230°C (450°F). Heat butter in a large frying pan over medium heat. Season breasts with salt and pepper. Brown breasts on meat side, then turn onto skin side and place in the oven. Roast for 10 minutes. (Breasts should be light pink in the middle; otherwise, they lose their delicate flavor.) Remove meat, set aside and keep warm.

Sauce:
300 mL (1¼ cups) game bird stock
(see recipe, page 10) or chicken broth
1 tsp cornstarch
3 Tbsp Madeira wine
Salt and pepper, to taste
1 Tbsp butter

Discard frying butter and place pan back on the stove. Pour in stock and boil down liquid to half the volume. Mix cornstarch with Madeira and gradually stir into stock. Adjust seasoning with salt and pepper, if necessary, and whisk butter into sauce.

Garnish:
200 g (7 oz) fresh wood mushrooms or
60 g (2 oz) dried (see Method, page 12)
1 Tbsp butter
1 shallot, finely chopped
Salt and pepper, to taste
1 Tbsp chopped parsley

Cut mushrooms into pieces if they are large. Heat butter over medium heat and sauté mushrooms with the shallot. Season with salt and pepper and sprinkle with parsley.

Serving suggestion

Slice breasts, pour a little sauce on warmed plates and arrange meat on top. Place garnish over meat and serve with wild rice mixed with corn kernels.

Substitute

Breast of guinea fowl.

Stuffed Pheasant Breasts with Madeira Sauce

Serves 4 to 6

2 pheasants, (4 breasts)

Debone pheasants (see Butchering). Prepare stock from carcasses (see recipe, page 10). Place breasts in the refrigerator for later use.

Stuffing:
4 deboned pheasant legs (use only thighs – drumsticks contain too many ligaments)
2 pheasant livers, trimmed (see Butchering)
1 slice white bread
1 Tbsp milk
1/2 tsp salt
Thyme, pinch
Nutmeg, pinch
Pepper, pinch
4 Tbsp whipping cream

Skin and debone pheasant thighs and remove ligaments. Soak bread with milk. Place all stuffing ingredients, except cream, into a food processor. While processing, gradually add the cream. Do not process too long; otherwise, stuffing will get too warm and crumbly. (If a food processor is not available, pass meat twice through the finest blade of a grinder. Place bowl over ice water and stir in cream.)

1 Tbsp olive oil
2 Tbsp butter
Salt and pepper, to taste

Place breasts meat side up on the counter. Open breasts from the middle (see picture, page 184), place stuffing on the center of the breasts and fold meat over giving the breasts their original shape.

Preheat oven to 200°C (400°F). Heat oil and butter in a large frying or roasting pan over medium heat. Season breasts on both sides with salt and pepper. Brown breasts on meat side, then turn onto the skin and place in the oven. Roast for about 20 minutes, basting occasionally. Remove meat, set aside on a plate and keep warm.

Sauce:
2 Tbsp dry white wine
4 Tbsp Madeira wine
125 mL (1/2 cup) game bird stock (see recipe, page 10) or chicken broth
125 mL (1/2 cup) whipping cream
1 Tbsp COLD butter
Salt and pepper, to taste

Discard frying oil and set pan back on the stove. Deglaze pan with white and Madeira wines, scraping off all solids from the bottom of the pan. Pour in stock and cream, bring to a boil. Boil down liquid to half the volume. Stir COLD butter into sauce and adjust seasoning with salt and pepper.

Serving suggestion

Slice breasts, pour a little sauce on warmed plates and arrange meat on top. Complement with wild rice and sweet corn or peas. (See picture, page 95.)

Substitute

Breast of guinea fowl.

94

Stuffed Pheasant Breasts with Madeira Sauce

Pheasant Breasts in Port Wine Sauce

Serves 4

2 pheasants, (4 breasts)
(see Butchering)
2 Tbsp butter
Salt and pepper, to taste

Preheat oven to 230°C (450°F). Heat butter in a heavy bottomed frying pan over medium heat. Season breasts with salt and pepper. Brown breasts on meat side, then turn onto skin sides and place in the oven. Roast for about 10 minutes, basting meat once during cooking. (Breasts should be light pink in the middle; otherwise, they lose their delicate flavor.) Remove meat, set aside on a plate to catch the juices and keep warm.

Sauce:
60 mL (¼ cup) port wine
125 mL (½ cup) game bird stock (see recipe, page 10) or chicken broth
2 Tbsp COLD butter

Discard frying oil and place pan over high heat. Deglaze pan with port and boil down liquid to half the volume. Add stock and meat juices and reduce until sauce becomes syrupy. Add COLD butter in small pieces, shaking pan back and forth. When all butter is incorporated, remove pan from heat.

Serving suggestion

Pour 1 Tbsp of sauce on each warmed plate. Slice breasts at an angle and fan out over sauce. Serve with fried potato rolls (see recipe, page 139) and spinach sautéed in butter.

Substitute

Guinea fowl.

Note: If only one pheasant is on hand, roast legs with the breasts. After removing the breasts, place legs on a plate and put back in the oven. Legs will be done by the time the sauce is finished.

Pheasant Pie

Serves 4 to 6

Puff pastry dough:
200 g (7 oz) puff pastry

(For recipe, see page 151) or frozen commercial dough can be used.

Broth:
2 pheasants (older birds can be used)
1.5 L (6 cups) water
1 tsp salt
1 medium onion, peeled and cut in half
4 cloves
2 bay leaves
10 peppercorns

Cut pheasants into quarters (see Butchering), wash and place with neck into a large saucepan. Add water and salt and bring to a boil. Add onion, cloves, bay leaves and peppercorns. Simmer for 50 minutes or until meat is tender. Remove meat, set aside and let cool. Strain broth.

Sauce:
3 Tbsp butter
4 Tbsp flour
500 mL (2 cups) broth (use broth in which pheasants were cooked)
125 mL (1/2 cup) whipping cream
3 medium carrots, peeled and sliced
200 g (7 oz) mushrooms, quartered
200 g (7 oz) peas, fresh or frozen

Melt butter in a saucepan over medium heat. Add flour and fry for a minute or two stirring constantly. Whisk in broth and bring to a boil. Add cream, carrots and mushrooms and boil gently for 15 minutes. Add peas and remove from heat.

Preheat oven to 200°C (400°F). Remove skin and bones from pheasants and cut meat into pieces. Place meat in an ovenproof glass or earthenware casserole and pour sauce over.

Roll out puff pastry on a floured surface to a thickness of about 3 mm (1/8 in.) and cover the casserole. Place in the oven and bake for 25 to 30 minutes or until pastry is golden brown.

Serving suggestion

Serve in the casserole dish. Complement with rice or boiled potatoes.

Substitute

3 Grouse, 4 partridges, 2 chickens, 1 rabbit or a small turkey 2 kg (4 lbs).

Note: This dish can be served without the pastry.

The leftover broth makes an excellent soup or stock.

Roast Pheasant with Bread Sauce

Serves 2 to 4

1 pheasant
Salt and pepper, to taste
2 Tbsp butter

Sauce:
250 mL (1 cup) milk
½ small onion, peeled
1 bay leaf
2 cloves
2 slices white bread, crusts removed
and cubed
Salt and pepper, to taste

Cranberry sauce (for garnish)

Serving suggestion

Substitute

Preheat oven to 230°C (450°F). Wash bird with cold water and dry with a paper towel. Tie pheasant (see Butchering) and rub with salt and pepper. Melt butter in frying or roasting pan and brush all over pheasant. Place on its side in the pan and put in the oven.

Total roasting time will be 35 minutes. Roast 15 minutes on each side, then turn bird breast side up for the last 5 minutes. Remove bird and set aside in a warm place for 10 minutes before carving.

While roasting pheasant, in a small saucepan, bring milk, onion, bay leaf and cloves to a boil. Set aside and let stand for 20 minutes. (This will mix the flavor of the herbs and onion into the milk.) Remove these ingredients with a slotted spoon and discard. Add bread to milk and bring back to a boil. Remove pan from the heat and whisk sauce until smooth. Adjust seasoning with salt and pepper.

Carve bird (see Butchering); pour sauce on warm plates and arrange meat on top. Complement with broccoli and potatoes and serve with cranberry sauce on the side.

Guinea fowl.

Note: When roasting 2 pheasants at the same time, total roasting time should be 40 minutes.

Wild Turkey Medallions in Basil Sauce

Serves 4

8 medallions from breast (see Butchering) 90 g (3 oz) each
2 Tbsp oil
2 Tbsp butter
Salt and pepper, to taste
Flour

Heat oil and butter in a heavy bottomed frying pan over medium heat. Season medallions with salt and pepper, dip into flour and shake off excess. Fry medallions until done. Remove meat, set aside on a plate to catch the juices and keep warm.

Sauce:
1 shallot or 1 Tbsp onion, finely chopped
60 mL (1/4 cup) dry white wine
125 mL (1/2 cup) chicken or turkey broth
250 mL (1 cup) whipping cream
1 tomato, peeled, seeds removed and diced
2 tsp chopped basil, fresh or 1 tsp dried
Salt and pepper, to taste

Add shallot to the pan and fry briefly. Deglaze pan with wine and boil down liquid to half the volume. Add broth and cream then reduce until a creamy consistency. Add tomato, meat juices and basil and bring back to a boil. Adjust seasoning with salt and pepper if necessary.

Serving suggestion

Place medallions on warmed plates and pour sauce over. Serve with fettucine or rice and any colorful vegetables.

Substitute

Schnitzel or medallions from domestic turkey, veal and pork.

99

Turkey Cordon Bleu

Serves 4

4 schnitzels from breast (see Butchering) 150 g (5 oz) each

4 slices ham
4 slices Swiss cheese
Salt, pinch
Pepper
Flour
2 eggs, beaten
Breadcrumbs

4 Tbsp peanut oil
4 Tbsp butter

1 lemon, cut into wedges (for garnish)

Serving suggestion

Substitute

Pound schnitzels very thin with a mallet between two sheets of plastic wrap. (This will prevent meat from breaking.)

In the center of the schnitzels, first place ham, then cheese (as shown below). Fold together, making sure cheese and ham are well covered with meat. Season with a little salt and pepper. Dip both sides of the meat into flour and shake off excess, then dip into the eggs and last into breadcrumbs.

Heat oil and butter in a large frying pan over medium heat. Fry meat on each side to a golden brown.

Place Cordon Bleu on warmed plates and garnish with lemon. Serve with fried potatoes or rice and a salad on the side. (See picture, page 101.)

Schnitzels from veal, pork and chicken breast.

Turkey Cordon Bleu

Wild Turkey with Hazelnut Stuffing

Serves 6 to 8

1 wild turkey 3.5 kg (7½ lbs)

Stuffing:
Meat from turkey thighs
Liver from turkey, cubed
1 slice white bread, cubed
1 egg
1 Tbsp whipped cream
2 Tbsp chopped onion
½ tsp salt
1 Tbsp chopped parsley
Pepper, pinch
Nutmeg, pinch
100 g (3½ oz) hazelnuts, coarsely
crushed

Sauce:
Salt and pepper
5 Tbsp flour
3 Tbsp butter
1 Tbsp tomato paste
1 small onion, coarsely chopped
1 small carrot, coarsely chopped
1 clove garlic
Thyme, pinch
Rosemary, pinch
20 peppercorns
Butter
125 mL (½ cup) dry white wine
500 mL (2 cups) water
250 mL (1 cup) whipping cream

Debone bird from the back (see Butchering). Remove thighs without cutting the skin and debone (see picture, page 103). Retain carcass for later use.

Pass thigh meat through the finest blade of a grinder and set aside. Place bread cubes in a large bowl. Beat egg and cream with a fork and pour over bread. Mix in all the other stuffing ingredients.

Preheat oven to 200°C (400°F). Season deboned turkey inside with salt and pepper. Place stuffing on the middle of the bird. Close with kitchen string, using a darning needle, to give back the turkey's original shape.

Chop the carcass and place into a large roasting pan. Rub bird with salt and pepper and place on top of the bones. Mix flour and butter together and roll out on a floured surface. Spread rolled mixture over breast and put in the oven (as shown on page 103). Total roasting time will be 2½ hours. After 30 minutes, lower oven temperature to 180°C (360°F). Roast for 60 minutes, then stir in tomato paste, onion, carrot, garlic, herbs and peppercorns. Roast for another 30 minutes. Remove pan from the oven and set turkey on an ovenproof plate. Take off butter and flour mixture and add to the bones. (This will thicken the sauce later.) Brush turkey with soft butter and put back in the oven for a further 30 minutes.

Meanwhile, place bones on stove over medium high heat. Pour in the wine and boil down liquid to half the volume, stirring constantly. Add water and a little salt and boil gently for 30 minutes. Strain into a saucepan, add cream and reduce to a creamy consistency. Adjust seasoning with salt and pepper if necessary.

Serving suggestion

Cut turkey in half, then slice. Arrange on warmed plates and serve sauce on the side. Complement with colorful vegetables and rice or potatoes.

Note: This dish can be reheated. When meat is cold, slice as mentioned above. Place on a buttered baking sheet, add a little water and cover with aluminum foil. Place in a 180°C (360°F) oven for about 30 minutes.

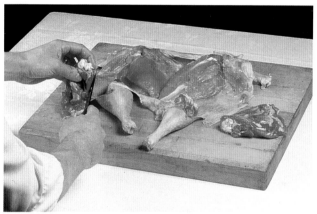

Removing thighs.

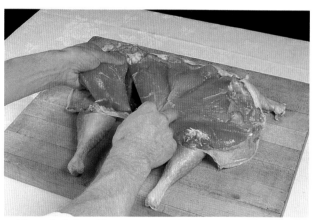

Fold tenderloin of breasts toward the legs, then make an incomplete cut at the thick end of breast to distribute the meat evenly on bird. Trim loose skin from around the bird.

Butter-flour mixture placed on top of the breasts.

Roast Wild Duckling in Port Wine Sauce

Serves 2

1 young duckling 800 g (28 oz)
Salt and pepper, to taste
½ orange, unpeeled
2 Tbsp butter

Sauce:
2 Tbsp brandy
60 mL (¼ cup) port wine
125 mL (½ cup) chicken broth
1 tsp cornstarch
1 Tbsp orange juice
Salt and pepper, to taste

Serving suggestion

Preheat oven to 220°C (425°F). Wash duckling with cold water and dry with a paper towel. Rub with salt and pepper and place orange in the cavity. Melt butter in a frying pan and brush all over duckling. Place on its side in the pan and put in the oven.

Total roasting time will be 35 minutes. Roast 15 minutes on each side, then turn bird breast side up for the last 5 minutes. Baste at each turn. Remove bird and set aside for 10 minutes.

Discard frying butter and place pan back on the stove. Deglaze pan with brandy and port. Add chicken broth and bring to a boil. Mix cornstarch with orange juice and slowly stir into broth. Adjust seasoning with salt and pepper. Carve duckling (see Butchering), catch all meat juices and stir into the sauce.

Arrange on warmed plates and pour sauce on top. Serve with wild rice mixed with peas and warmed half peaches.

Duck Breasts Marinated in Soya Sauce and White Wine

Serves 4

2 wild ducks, (4 breasts)
(see Butchering)

Marinade:
125 mL (½ cup) dry white wine
3 Tbsp soya sauce
10 peppercorns, crushed
5 juniper berries, crushed
Thyme, pinch
2 Tbsp brown sugar
1 Tbsp oil

Mix all ingredients of the marinade in a bowl and place in breasts. Place in the refrigerator and marinate for one to two days. Remove meat, discard marinade and pat meat dry with a paper towel.

2 Tbsp olive oil

1 green onion, chopped
(for garnish)

Preheat oven to 230°C (450°F). Heat oil in a large frying pan over high heat. Brown breasts on meat side, then turn onto the skin side and place in the oven. Roast for about 10 minutes (depending on the size of the breasts). (Breasts should be pink in the middle; otherwise, they become too dry.) Remove meat and set aside on a plate to catch the juices. Let stand at least 5 minutes before carving.

Serving suggestion

Remove skin from breasts and discard. Cut breasts into thin slices and arrange on warmed plates. Pour meat juices on top and sprinkle with green onions. Serve with rice mixed with fried mushrooms.

Substitute

Domestic duck and wild goose breasts. (Cooking time for goose breasts is about 25 minutes.)

Deboned Stuffed Duck

Serves 4

1 wild duck 800 g (28 oz)

Debone bird from the back (see Butchering).

Stuffing:
1 liver from duck or 2 from chicken
2 Tbsp chopped onion
1 Tbsp butter
1 medium apple, peeled, cored and cubed
1 slice white bread, cubed
1 Tbsp chopped parsley
1 egg
200 g (7 oz) duck or other game fowl or chicken, ground
$\frac{1}{2}$ tsp salt
Pepper, pinch
Nutmeg, pinch

Trim liver (see Butchering) and cut into small cubes. Sauté onion in butter for a minute, add liver and sauté briefly. Place all stuffing ingredients in a bowl and mix thoroughly.

Season duck inside with salt and pepper. Place stuffing on the middle and close with kitchen string, using a darning needle.

Salt and pepper, to taste
Marjoram, pinch
125 mL ($\frac{1}{2}$ cup) water

Preheat oven to 180°C (360°F). Rub duck with a little salt, pepper and marjoram. Place with water into a roasting pan and put in the oven. Roast for about $1\frac{1}{2}$ hours, basting occasionally. Remove bird, set aside and keep warm.

125 mL ($\frac{1}{2}$ cup) whipping cream

Skim fat from roasting juices. Place pan on the stove, pour in the cream and bring to a boil. Boil down sauce to one-third of the volume. Adjust seasoning with salt and pepper.

Serving suggestion

Slice duck, arrange on warmed plates or platter and pour sauce over. Complement with peas and parsley potatoes.

Substitute

Domestic duck and wild goose. (For goose, double stuffing recipe and cook for $2\frac{1}{2}$ hours.)

Stuffed Roast Duck

Serves 2

1 wild duck about 800 g (28 oz)

Stuffing:
1 Tbsp butter
1 small onion, coarsely chopped
Liver from duck, cubed
1 medium apple, peeled, cored and cubed

Salt and pepper, to taste
1 tsp marjoram
250 mL (1 cup) water
1 Tbsp butter

1 tsp cornstarch
2 Tbsp apple juice

Serving suggestion

Substitute

Preheat oven to 190°C (375°F). Wash duck inside and out with cold water and dry with a paper towel.

Heat butter in a frying pan and sauté onion for a minute, add liver and apple and sauté briefly. Fill cavity with stuffing and close with small skewers or toothpicks and kitchen string (see Butchering).

Rub bird with salt, pepper and marjoram and place in a roasting pan, just a little larger than the duck. Add half of the water and put in the oven. Roasting time will be 1 hour. Roast 20 minutes on its back, breast side up, then 20 minutes on each side. Baste at each turn. Remove bird and place on an ovenproof plate, breast side up. Brush bird all over with butter and put back in the oven to crispen the skin.

Place pan on the stove, skim off fat, leaving roasting juices. Add remaining water and bring to a boil, scraping off all solids from the bottom of the pan. Mix cornstarch with the apple juice and stir in slowly to thicken the sauce.

Carve duck (see Butchering) and serve with stuffing. Complement with fried potatoes. Serve sauce on the side.

Domestic duck. (Prick skin with a needle on domestic duck so fat can escape while roasting.)

Wild Duck Casserole

Serves 4

2 wild ducks about 800 g (28 oz) each
2 Tbsp butter
Salt and pepper, to taste

1 medium turnip
4 slices bacon, cut into strips
200 g (7 oz) mushrooms, quartered
2 Tbsp brandy
60 mL (¼ cup) game bird stock (see recipe, page 10) or chicken broth

Serving suggestion

Substitute

Preheat oven to 230°C (450°F). Heat butter in a frying or roasting pan over medium heat. Rub ducks inside and out with salt and pepper. Brush with melted butter and put in the oven. Roast for 40 minutes, basting occasionally. Remove birds and set aside on a plate.

Peel turnip, cut into balls (like melon balls) or cubes. Cook for 5 minutes in salted water, strain and set aside. Fry bacon over medium high heat in frying pan. Once bacon starts to get crisp, add mushrooms and fry for a few minutes. Remove with a slotted spoon and set aside.

Lower oven temperature to 190°C (375°F). Cut off legs and breasts and place in a casserole. Pour brandy, stock and meat juices over meat and add turnip, bacon and mushrooms. Cover and place in the oven for 30 minutes or until meat is tender.

Serve in the casserole dish and complement with a salad.

Domestic ducks. (Before placing domestic ducks in casserole, remove most of the fat.)

Braised Goose in Red Wine

Serves 4

1 Canada goose, skin removed (an older goose can be used)
2 Tbsp oil
2 Tbsp butter
Salt and pepper, to taste
Flour

Preheat oven to 180°C (360°F). Cut bird into pieces, wash with cold water and pat dry with a paper towel. Heat oil and butter in a heavy bottomed saucepan over medium heat. Season meat pieces with salt and pepper, dip into flour and shake off excess. Brown meat on both sides. Remove and set aside.

1 small onion, coarsely chopped
1 clove garlic
1 small carrot, coarsely chopped
1 tsp thyme
Rosemary, pinch
20 black peppercorns
2 cloves
2 Tbsp flour
250 mL (1 cup) dry red wine
250 mL (1 cup) game bird stock (see recipe, page 10) or chicken broth

In the same pan, add all vegetables and herbs and fry until onion is soft. Stir in flour and fry for a minute. Deglaze pan with wine, bring to a boil and scrape off all solids from the bottom of the pan. Add stock and return meat pieces to the sauce. Cover and braise in the oven for 1½ hours or until meat is tender. Remove meat and place in a serving dish.

Place pan back on the stove. Sauce should have a nice consistency (cream-like); otherwise, boil down or add liquid as needed. Adjust seasonings as desired. Strain sauce through a sieve over goose, pressing vegetables to get all their juices.

Serving suggestion

Serve goose with mashed potatoes or servietten knoedle (see recipe, page 138). Complement with mushrooms fried with bacon strips or young peas.

Substitute

2 wild ducks, skinned. (If using domestic goose, skin and remove all fat.)

Roast Wild Goose Breasts with Bacon

Serves 4 to 6

1 goose, (2 breasts) skin removed (see Butchering)
Pepper, to taste
6 juniper berries, finely crushed
Salt, pinch
8 slices bacon

Preheat oven to 220°C (425°F). Season goose breasts with pepper, juniper berries and very little salt — (bacon is already salted). Wrap each breast with 4 slices of bacon. Set in a frying or roasting pan so that the ends of the bacon meet at the bottom and will not unfold when cooking. Place in the oven for about 25 minutes (breasts should be pink in the middle). Remove breasts, set aside on a plate and let stand 5 minutes before slicing.

Serving suggestion

Cut breasts into finger thick slices and place with bacon on warmed plates or platter. Pour meat juices on top. Serve with creamed brussel sprouts and mashed potatoes.

Substitute

Wild duck breasts (cooking time is about 15 minutes).

Roast Stuffed Canada Goose

Serves 6

1 Canada goose

Stuffing:
1 egg
60 mL (¼ cup) whipping cream
5 slices white bread, cubed
1 Tbsp butter
1 small onion, chopped
1 large apple, peeled, cored and cubed
Liver from goose or from 2 chickens,
trimmed (see Butchering) and cubed
1 Tbsp chopped parsley
Salt and pepper, to taste
Nutmeg, pinch

Marjoram
250 mL (1 cup) water
1 Tbsp butter

2 tsp cornstarch
1 Tbsp cold water

Serving suggestion

Substitute

Wash goose inside and out with cold water and dry with a paper towel.

Mix egg with cream and pour over bread. Melt butter in a small frying pan over medium heat. Fry onion until soft, add apple and liver and sauté briefly. Remove from heat, place in a bowl and mix in all the other stuffing ingredients.

Preheat oven 175°C (350°F). Place stuffing in cavity and close with small skewers or toothpicks and kitchen string (see Butchering).

Rub goose with salt, pepper and marjoram. Place bird in a roasting pan, just a little larger than goose. Add water and put in the oven. Total roasting time will be about 2 hours and 45 minutes. Roast 45 minutes on its back, breast side up, then 45 minutes on each side. Baste occasionally. Raise oven temperature to 190°C (375°F). Remove bird and place on an ovenproof plate, breast side up. Brush bird all over with butter and place back in the oven for 30 minutes to crispen the skin. Remove bird and set aside.

Meanwhile, place pan on the stove, skim off fat, leaving only roasting juices. Bring to a boil and thicken with cornstarch mixed with water. (Juices should only be thickened slightly; if there are not enough juices, add chicken broth.)

Carve goose, arrange with stuffing on warmed plates or platter. Serve goose juices on the side. Complement with a small salad or red cabbage (see recipe, page 135) or sauerkraut (see recipe, page 139) or creamed brussel sprouts. (See picture, page 111.)

Domestic goose. (Prick skin with a needle so fat can escape while bird is roasting.)

Note: Keep roasting fat to give a nice flavor when cooking sauerkraut or red cabbage.

GROUND GAME, SAUSAGES AND LEFTOVER MEAT

GROUND GAME

Much of the front quarter, and any parts or trimmings which are free of fat, blood clots and tough ligaments, can yield good quality ground meat. This is suitable for sausages, burger patties, meat pies and loaves and meat sauces.

Game meat in general is so lean that one part fatty pork trimmings should be mixed with every two parts of game meat. Beef can be used, but pork gives a better flavor. Since pork does not freeze as well as game, freezing ground game/pork mixtures for more than six months is not recommended. For best results, combine pork and game shortly before cooking. The two should be mixed together while grinding, feeding them into the grinder alternately. It is important that the grinder blades are very sharp as the friction from dull blades will heat the meat and produce poorly textured ground meat.

SAUSAGES

The meat from any big game animal can be used for sausages but elk meat provides the best results. It should be trimmed of blood clots and tough ligaments.

Synthetic or natural casings, which can be obtained from a butcher, can be used for sausages. Casings should be soaked in lukewarm water for 30 minutes before using, to make them flexible. Natural casings come packed in salt; the leftovers can be salted again and kept in a sealed glass jar in a refrigerator for a year.

Virtually any kind of sausage can be made at home with a simple meat grinder, sausage stuffer and a smoker (if available). This section features some simple recipes, and with experience and experimentation, you will be able to make your own custom sausages.

Shepherd's Pie

Serves 4 to 6

400 g (14 oz) game meat
200 g (7 oz) fatty pork shoulder
4 medium potatoes
2 Tbsp butter
1 small onion, chopped
Salt and pepper, to taste
300 mL (1¼ cups) corn kernels
60 mL (¼ cup) whipping cream
1 tsp cornstarch
2 Tbsp butter
2 egg yolks

Serving suggestion

Substitute

Preheat oven to 200°C (400°F). Cook potatoes in salted water. Grind meat with pork. Heat butter in a large frying pan over medium heat. Sauté onion until soft, add ground meats, season with salt and pepper and fry until cooked. Spread meat on the bottom of an ovenproof dish and set aside. In the same pan, add corn kernels, cream and cornstarch. Bring to a boil, stirring constantly until very thick, then pour over meat. Mash hot potatoes and stir in butter, egg yolks, salt and pepper; spread over corn. Place in the oven for about 20 minutes.

Serve in the ovenproof dish and complement with a salad or pickled vegetables such as beets, carrots and onions.

Lamb and beef. (Do not add pork.)

Note: Shepherd's pie can be made with leftover game roast. A can of cream-style corn may be used instead of corn kernels, cream and cornstarch mixture.

Shepherd's Pie

Game Burgers

Serves 4 to 6

400 g (14 oz) game meat
150 g (5 oz) fatty pork belly or shoulder
1 egg
2 Tbsp milk
2 Tbsp breadcrumbs
2 Tbsp chopped onion
1 Tbsp Dijon mustard
Salt and pepper, to taste

2 Tbsp oil

Grind meat with pork and place in a large bowl. Beat egg with milk, add breadcrumbs and soak for a few minutes, add to the meat and mix in all the other ingredients.

Shape into patties. Barbecue or heat oil in a frying pan and fry until done.

Meat Loaf

Serves 4 to 6

400 g (14 oz) game meat
150 g (5 oz) fatty pork belly or shoulder
1 Tbsp butter
1 small onion, chopped
1 clove garlic, crushed
2 slices bacon, cut into strips
1 egg
2 Tbsp milk
3 slices white bread, crusts removed and cubed
2 Tbsp chopped parsley
1 1/2 tsp salt
1 tsp pepper
Nutmeg, pinch
Butter (for baking sheet)

Preheat oven to 190°C (375°F). Grind meat with pork and place in a large bowl. Heat butter in a frying pan over medium heat. Fry onion, garlic and bacon until onion is soft, and set aside. Beat egg with milk and pour over bread cubes. Add to the meat and mix in all the other ingredients.

Form a loaf and place on a buttered baking sheet. Bake in the oven for 45 to 60 minutes or until meat is done.

Serving suggestion

Slice loaf and serve with peas, carrots and parsley potatoes or a salad. For variety, place boiled eggs or whole dill pickles inside the loaf, along the middle, and bake.

Substitute

Beef. (Do not add pork.)

Game Loaf in a Crust
Serves 4 to 6

Short Pastry Dough:
300 g (2 cups) all-purpose flour
½ tsp salt
150 g (5 oz) butter or lard
1 egg
3 Tbsp milk (approximately)

Have all dough ingredients at room temperature. Place flour in a large bowl and sprinkle with salt. Cut butter into flour and mix, with your hands or a fork, until crumbly. Beat egg with milk, add to flour and mix in quickly (do not over-mix the dough; otherwise, it will lose flakiness when baked). Cover with plastic wrap or a damp cloth and place in the refrigerator.

Filling:
400 g (14 oz) game meat
200 g (7 oz) fatty pork
2 Tbsp butter
1 small onion, chopped
1 red bell pepper, chopped
125 g (4 oz) Swiss cheese, grated
1 Tbsp green peppercorns
Salt and pepper, to taste
2 Tbsp chopped parsley
1 Tbsp brandy
2 eggs
125 mL (½ cup) breadcrumbs

1 egg yolk mixed with 1 tsp water

Grind meat with pork. Heat butter in a large frying pan over medium heat. Fry onion and bell pepper until soft. Add the ground meats and fry until cooked. Remove meat, place in a large bowl and mix in all the other filling ingredients.

Assembling Loaf:
Preheat oven to 190°C (375°F). On a floured surface, roll dough to about a 35 cm (14 in.) square and a thickness of 3 mm (1/8 in.). From the square, cut a piece of dough about 15 cm (6 in.) wide and place on a lightly floured baking sheet. Arrange meat on top, leaving 10 mm (½ in.) space around the edges. Brush edges with some of the egg yolk mixture. Cover with the remaining dough, pressing edges together with a fork. Brush top crust with remaining yolk mixture. Poke holes in the dough with a fork to allow steam to escape while baking. Put loaf in the oven and bake for about 35 minutes.

Serving suggestion

Cut loaf into serving portions and serve with mushroom sauce (see recipe, page 16). Complement with vegetables or a salad on the side.

Substitute

Ground meat from beef, lamb, pork and veal. (Do not add pork.)

Note: This recipe can also be made in a pie plate.

116

Game Pie

Serves 4 to 6

Short Pastry Dough:

(For recipe, see page 116.)

Filling:
300 g (10 oz) game meat
150 g (5 oz) fatty pork belly
50 g (2 oz) chicken liver, trimmed
1 Tbsp butter
1 shallot, chopped
100 g (3½ oz) mushrooms, sliced
2 Tbsp brandy
2 Tbsp Madeira wine
1 tsp salt
½ tsp pepper, freshly ground
Nutmeg, pinch
Thyme, pinch
60 mL (¼ cup) whipping cream

Trim meat of most ligaments and silver skin. Heat butter in a frying pan over medium heat. Sauté shallot briefly, add mushrooms and fry for a few minutes more. Pour in brandy and Madeira, boil down until nearly dry, set aside and let cool. Grind meat, pork, liver and mushroom mixture through the finest blade of a grinder. Place in a large bowl and mix in all the other ingredients.

Assembling Pie:
Preheat oven to 190°C (375°F). Reserving sufficient dough for a cover, roll remaining dough on a floured surface and line a 23 cm (9 in.) pie plate. Fill with the meat mixture and cover with the reserved rolled dough. Press edges together with a fork and cut a small hole in the middle of the top crust to allow steam to escape. Decorate with the remaining dough (optional). Bake for 45 to 55 minutes or until golden brown.

Serving suggestion

Serve with cranberry sauce and a salad with vinaigrette dressing (see recipe, page 16).

Substitute

Veal and beef.

Game Strudel

Serves 6

Strudel Dough:

Filling:
600 g (21 oz) game meat, ground
1 Tbsp butter
1 small onion, chopped
4 slices bacon, cut into strips
1 clove garlic, crushed
1 bunch spinach
60 mL (¼ cup) whipping cream
35 g (¼ cup) breadcrumbs
1 egg
Salt and pepper, to taste
Nutmeg, pinch

2 Tbsp melted butter

Serving suggestion

Substitute

(For recipe, see page 146.)
Prepare and pull strudel dough as shown on page 147.

Preheat oven to 190°C (375°F). Heat butter in a large frying pan over medium high heat. Fry onion, bacon and garlic until onion is soft. Add ground meat and fry until cooked. Place this mixture in a large bowl. Put the pan back on the stove, add spinach and cream and cook to a syrupy consistency, set aside and let cool. Coarsely chop the spinach mixture, add to the meat and mix in all the remaining ingredients.

Assembling Strudel:
Spread filling on one-fourth of the stretched dough. Brush remaining stretched dough with melted butter. Roll strudel by lifting cloth from the meat side (as shown on page 147). Place strudel on a buttered baking sheet, ends down, and brush top with melted butter. (If baking sheet is not long enough lay out strudel in an "L" or "U" shape.) Bake for 40 minutes or until golden brown.

Serve with mushroom sauce (see recipe, page 16) and colorful vegetables. Without sauce, serve a salad with a creamy dressing.

Ground meat from beef, lamb, pork and veal.

Cabbage Roll-Ups

Serves 4 to 6

1 medium Savoy, green or red cabbage

In a large saucepan, a little larger than the cabbage, bring salted water to a boil. Remove core and place cabbage, top first, into boiling water. Boil for about 10 minutes, loosening leaves with a fork. Remove pan from heat, drain cabbage and place it under cold running water. Once leaves are cold, remove and place on a paper towel to dry. Reserve 10 to 12 of the larger leaves and cut remaining leaves into fine strips.

Stuffing:
500 g (1 lb) game meat, ground
4 slices bacon, cut into strips
10 green onions, chopped
Small inner leaves of cabbage
2 Tbsp chopped parsley
125 mL (1/2 cup) whipping cream
Salt and pepper, to taste
Thyme, pinch

Over medium high heat, sauté bacon and green onions for a few minutes. Add cabbage strips and parsley, sauté briefly and add cream. Reduce to a syrupy consistency, set aside and let cool. Place in a bowl and mix in remaining stuffing ingredients.

Season reserved leaves with salt and pepper and fill each with about 3 Tbsp of stuffing. Fold in sides and roll up. Secure with toothpicks or tie crosswise with kitchen string (as shown below).

2 Tbsp butter
125 mL (1/2 cup) chicken or beef broth
125 mL (1/2 cup) whipping cream
3 Tbsp sour cream
1 Tbsp flour

1 Tbsp chopped parsley (for garnish)

Heat butter in a large frying pan over medium heat. Quickly fry the rolls on all sides. Add broth, cover and braise slowly for about 45 minutes on top of the stove or in the oven at 180°C (360°F). Meanwhile, in a bowl, whisk whipping cream, sour cream and flour. Remove rolls, set aside and keep warm. Stir the cream mixture into boiling broth and simmer for 15 minutes. Adjust seasoning with salt and pepper if necessary.

Serving suggestion

Place cabbage rolls on warmed plates or platter, pour a little sauce on top and sprinkle with chopped parsley. Complement with fried potatoes or roesti (see recipe, page 134) and serve remaining sauce on the side.

Substitute

Ground meat from beef, lamb and veal.

On reserved cabbage leaves, thin main vein to prevent splitting while rolling.

Roll and secure.

Game Tourtière (Pie)

Serves 4 to 6

Pie Dough:
250 g (2 cups) pastry flour
Salt, pinch
200 g (7 oz) lard
1 egg
1 Tbsp vinegar
125 mL (½ cup) water

Have all dough ingredients at room temperature. Pour flour into a large bowl and sprinkle with salt. Cut lard into flour and mix, with hands or a fork until crumbly. Beat egg in vinegar and water, add to flour and mix in quickly. Cover with plastic wrap or a damp cloth and place in the refrigerator.

Filling:
350 g (12 oz) game meat
150 g (5 oz) fatty pork belly
4 slices bacon, cut into strips
1 small onion, chopped
1 clove garlic, chopped
1 stalk celery, chopped
250 mL (1 cup) water
1 medium potato
1 medium apple
Salt and pepper, to taste
Nutmeg, pinch
Mace, pinch
2 bay leaves
1 tsp cinnamon
Cloves, pinch

Grind meat with pork through the finest blade of a meat grinder. Place saucepan over medium heat and fry bacon, onion, garlic and celery until onion is soft. Stir in ground meats, pour water over and stir again. Peel potato and apple, grate coarsely and stir into the meat. Add remaining spices and cook slowly for about 30 minutes, stirring occasionally. When most of the liquid has evaporated, remove from the heat, discard bay leaves and set aside.

1 egg yolk mixed with 1 Tbsp water

Assembling Tourtière:
Preheat oven to 190°C (375°F). Reserving sufficient dough for a cover, roll remaining dough on a floured surface and line a 23 cm (9 in.) pie plate. Add filling and cover with the reserved rolled dough. Press edges together with a fork and cut a small hole in the middle of the top crust to allow steam to escape. Brush top crust with egg yolk mixture and bake for 30 to 45 minutes or until brown. (See picture, page 112.)

Serving suggestion

Serve with a salad or pickled vegetables such as beets and onions.

Substitute

Any type of meat mixed with pork (⅔ meat with ⅓ pork).

Spaghetti Sauce

Serves 8

500 g (1 lb) game meat, ground
4 Tbsp olive oil
2 medium onions, chopped
1 small green bell pepper, chopped
1 stalk celery, chopped
2 cloves garlic, crushed
150 g (5 oz) mushrooms, sliced
(optional)
156 mL (5½ fl oz) tomato paste
540 mL (19 fl oz) tomato juice
796 mL (28 fl oz) peeled tomatoes
2 bay leaves
1 tsp thyme
1 tsp oregano
1 tsp sweet basil
1 tsp salt
1 tsp pepper
1 tsp sugar

Heat oil in a large saucepan over medium high heat. Fry all vegetables until onions are soft. Add meat, stir in tomato paste and fry for a few more minutes. Pour in tomato juice and peeled tomatoes, then bring mixture to a boil. Add remaining ingredients and simmer slowly for 1½ hours, partially covered.

Serving suggestion

Place spaghetti on warmed plates, pour sauce on top and sprinkle with grated Parmesan cheese. Complement with a salad on the side.

Substitute

Ground beef and veal.

Note: Sauce may be used on macaroni, fettucine, lasagna, etc. The sauce may be frozen.

Grilled Game Sausages

1 kg (2 lbs) lean big game meat
500 g (1 lb) fat pork trimmings
1½ Tbsp salt
½ tsp cure
1 clove garlic, finely crushed
½ Tbsp paprika
2 tsp white pepper, ground
1 tsp coriander, ground
125 mL (½ cup) ice water
Pork casing

Serving suggestion

Meat has to be well-chilled and must be trimmed of blood clots and tough ligaments. Grind meat and pork using the finest blade of a grinder. Mix thoroughly with spices and ice water until mixture binds well together.

Stuff into casing; link or cut into serving size pieces. Place in the refrigerator for at least 3 hours before cooking (to allow time for curing). Sausages will keep for 2 to 3 days, chilled.

Cook sausages on a barbecue grill and serve with potato salad.

Note: Sausages can also be smoked before grilling to add flavor.

Make sure meat is ground not crushed. Meat should flow freely from blade; otherwise, blade is not tight or sharp enough.

Soak casings 30 minutes in warm water before using. Have a little sausage stuffing showing at the end of tube. Pour water into casing, then feed all the casing on the tube.

Game Bratwurst (Breakfast Sausage)

1 kg (2 lbs) lean big game meat
500 g (1 lb) fat pork trimmings
1½ Tbsp salt
1 tsp onion salt
1 tsp mace, ground
1 tsp marjoram
1 tsp white pepper, ground
125 mL (½ cup) milk
Pork or lamb casing

Serving suggestion

Meat has to be well-chilled and must be trimmed of blood clots and tough ligaments. Grind game meat and pork through the finest blade of a grinder. Mix thoroughly with spices and milk until mixture binds well together.

Stuff into casings and link or cut into serving size pieces. Sausage will keep for 2 to 3 days in the refrigerator.

Fry sausages slowly in oil or grill until done.

Bratwurst can be used for breakfast or supper. Serve with fried potatoes, sauerkraut and mustard.

Note: This sausage is made without cure and therefore, will not have a pink color after cooking.

Stuff sausage by holding casing up with one hand. Do not stuff too tight in order to link sausages afterwards. (A hand grinder will make stuffing easier since it has a large feeder opening.)

Link sausages to about 100 g (3 oz) turning each in opposite directions so they will not unlink when hanging to smoke.

123

Bavarian Game Meat Loaf

1 kg (2 lbs) lean big game meat
500 g (1 lb) fat pork trimmings
1½ Tbsp salt
1 tsp onion powder
½ tsp cure
1 tsp white pepper, ground
1 tsp coriander, ground
1 tsp mustard powder
1 tsp nutmeg, ground
2 Tbsp potato flour (starch)
2 Tbsp milk
500 mL (2 cups) ice water

Serving suggestion

Meat has to be well-chilled and must be trimmed of blood clots and tough ligaments.

Pass meat through the finest blade of a grinder. Sprinkle meat with all spices. Mix flour with milk and pour over meat; add ice water. Kneed all ingredients thoroughly. Place in the refrigerator for 3 to 4 hours (to allow time to cure). Process briefly in a food processor to a semi-fine texture. (Do half the mixture at a time.)

Grease a loaf pan with lard or butter. Fill to the top with the meat mixture, avoiding air pockets. Bake in a 160°C (325°F) for 1½ hours. Loaf should have a nice brown crust on the top.

Serve hot with potato salad and mustard or use cold for sandwiches.

Note: If food processor is not available, pass meat a second time through the grinder after refrigerating.

Game Salami

2.2 kg (5 lbs) elk or venison, well trimmed (meat from older animal should be used)
600 g (23 oz) firm pork back fat
3½ Tbsp salt
2 tsp cure
2 tsp raw sugar
1 Tbsp white pepper, ground
1 Tbsp black peppercorns, crushed
1 tsp allspice
1 clove garlic, finely crushed (optional)
125 mL (½ cup) dry red wine
Beef middles, pork or fibrous casing

Cut meat into large cubes and place for 2 to 3 hours in the freezer. Take out and grind all meat through a 6 mm (¼ in.) blade. Add all the spices and wine and mix thoroughly until meat binds together. Stuff mixture into casing.

Before smoking, hang sausages in a cool place for 1 week. (This will allow proper curing.) Smoke cold, not over 20°C (70°F) for 2 to 3 days or until salami has a nice color (golden brown). Remove from smoker and hang to dry in a cool place (not over 15°C (60°F) for at least 4 weeks).

Salami can be dried further and will keep for months in a cool place.

Note: At home, salami can only be made properly during the cool months, since cool temperatures are needed for smoking and curing.

Using a thin calibre casing, such as pork casing, will allow the sausage to dry more quickly enabling it to be eaten sooner and giving it less chance to spoil.

Use meat from older animals; this meat is dryer and has more meat acids (a natural preservative) than meat from young animals.

Make sure meat grinder is chilled, clean and in best working order, so meat will not overheat during grinding.

When stuffing salami, work with clean dry hands and make sure casing is stuffed tightly without air pockets. (Puncture any air pockets with a needle.)

Salami has to dry slowly from the inside; check sausage carefully for the first two weeks of drying. The white coating on the outside shows that salami is drying properly. If outside starts to feel hard and dry, spray with water or wipe with a wet clean cloth so sausage will be able to breathe again.

If conditions are not right, take sausage to a reliable butcher for smoking and drying.

Smoked Venison

2 kg (4 lbs)

2 kg (4 lbs) venison or elk meat from inside (top) – outside (bottom) round or round (see Butchering)
2 Tbsp salt
1 Tbsp cure
2 tsp raw sugar
2 tsp white pepper, ground
10 juniper berries, crushed

Remove silver skin and all ligaments. Mix salt, cure, sugar, pepper and juniper berries. Rub meat well on all sides with the spice mixture and pack tight in a clean container (not metal). Sprinkle leftover spices over meat. (Make sure to use all the salt mixture.) Cover with a wooden lid or a dinner plate and place for 1 week in the refrigerator, turning meat every second day.

Rinse meat with cold water and hang to dry for at least one day in a cool place. Dust with pepper and smoke cold, (not over 20°C (70°F)). Meat should be hung in a cool place to dry for at least 4 weeks. Smoked venison will keep for months in a cool room.

Serving suggestion

Cut meat, paper thin, with a meat slicer, and serve on buttered rye bread or with melon, apple, papaya fruit or salad.

Game Jerky I

1 kg (2 lbs) venison, elk or moose
1 Tbsp salt
1 tsp cure
1 tsp raw sugar
½ tsp pepper, ground
1 small clove garlic, crushed

Trim meat of all ligaments and fat. Cut meat into 1 cm x 2½ cm x 15 cm (½ in. x 1 in. x 6 in.) strips.

In a bowl, mix salt, cure, sugar, pepper and garlic. Rub each strip of meat, using all the salt mixture. Cover with a wooden lid or a dinner plate and place in the refrigerator for 3 days.

Remove meat and hang to dry in a cool place for 3 or 4 hours. Place meat into a smoker and smoke for 1 day. Dry for another 3 or 4 days, hanging the meat in a cool airy place. Meat should be dry but supple enough to bend without breaking.

Note: If smoker is not available, place meat strips on an oven rack. Dry at 40°C (100°F) for 3 to 4 hours, holding oven door open with a wooden spoon. Hang for a few days in a cool place to dry further.

Game Jerky II

1 kg (2 lbs) venison, elk or moose

For trimming and cutting, see above recipe.

Marinade:
125 mL (½ cup) soya sauce
125 mL (½ cup) dry red wine
1 Tbsp fresh ginger, chopped
1 tsp raw sugar
1 tsp cure

Mix all ingredients of the marinade in a bowl, then add the meat. Marinate for 3 days in the refrigerator. Remove meat and discard marinade.

See directions as above.

Substitute

Beef.

Note: Jerky will keep for months in a glass jar covered with a perforated lid.

Game Soufflé

Serves 4

300 g (10 oz) leftover game or game
fowl roast
500 mL (2 cups) milk
1/2 small onion, peeled
1 bay leaf
2 cloves
Butter and breadcrumbs (to prepare
soufflé dish)
2 Tbsp soft butter mixed with
3 Tbsp flour
5 egg yolks
Salt and pepper, to taste
Paprika, pinch
1 tsp dry mustard
100 g (3 1/2 oz) Swiss cheese, grated
5 egg whites
Milk (to thin sauce)

4 Tbsp cranberry jelly (for garnish)

Serving suggestion

In a saucepan, place milk, onion, bay leaf and cloves. Bring to a boil and set aside. Meanwhile, grind meat through the coarsest blade of a grinder and set aside. Brush soufflé dish with butter and cover butter with breadcrumbs.

Preheat oven to 190°C (375°F). With a slotted spoon, remove onion, bay leaf and cloves from milk and discard. Set pan over medium high heat, stir in flour and butter mixture and bring to a boil for a minute, stirring constantly. Pour half of the sauce over meat and set the other half aside for later use. Stir egg yolks, salt, pepper, paprika, mustard and cheese into the meat. Whip egg whites to a peak and fold into meat mixture. Pour into one large soufflé dish, filling until three-quarters full. Place on a baking sheet and bake in the oven for about 50 minutes. Meanwhile, place remaining sauce back on the stove, add milk and simmer for 30 minutes (sauce should keep a creamy consistency). When soufflé is baked, serve immediately. (See picture, page 129.)

Spoon soufflé onto serving plates and pour sauce on top. Serve with steamed broccoli and carrots. Complement with cranberry jelly.

Game Soufflé

Game Salad

Serves 4

300 g (10 oz) leftover game or game
fowl roast
2 oranges

125 mL (¹/₂ cup) mayonnaise
1 tsp dry English mustard
1 Tbsp cranberry jelly

Serving suggestion

Cut meat into fine strips. Peel oranges with a knife and cut out
segments between membranes. Set aside and keep for
decorating. Squeeze juice from orange membrane and set aside.

In a large bowl, mix mayonnaise, mustard, cranberry jelly and
orange juice. Toss the meat in the mayonnaise mixture.

Arrange meat neatly on salad leaves. Decorate with orange
sections, sprinkle with chopped nuts (optional) and serve with
toast. Meat salad can also be used in sandwiches.

Game Salad with Game Salad Sandwiches

130

Game Omelettes

Serves 4 to 6

300 g (10 oz) leftover game or game
fowl roast
2 Tbsp butter
1 small onion, chopped
200 g (7 oz) mushrooms, sliced
125 mL (½ cup) whipping cream
1 Tbsp chopped parsley
Salt and pepper, to taste
1 tsp cornstarch
2 Tbsp dry white wine
12 eggs
4 Tbsp butter

Serving suggestion

Cut meat into small cubes and set aside. Heat butter in a frying pan over medium heat. Fry onion and mushrooms until soft. Add meat, cream and parsley; season with salt and pepper and bring to a boil. Mix cornstarch with wine and stir gradually into the meat mixture. Reduce to a very thick consistency and set aside.

Beat the eggs thoroughly, adding a little salt and pepper. Heat 1 Tbsp butter (per omelette) in a non-stick frying pan. Fry eggs on one side only. When top is set cover with the meat mixture and fold omelette in half. Serve immediately. Makes 2 to 4 omelettes (depending on the size of the pan).

Serve with salad or fried potatoes.

SERVING SUGGESTIONS

Scalloped Potatoes

Serves 6

750 g (26 oz) potatoes
1 clove garlic
Butter (for gratin dish)
Salt and pepper, to taste
250 mL (1 cup) coffee cream
4 Tbsp grated cheese, Parmesan and/or Swiss

Cut garlic in half, rub sides and bottom of a gratin or shallow baking dish, then grease well with butter.

Preheat oven to 200°C (400°F). Peel potatoes and wash. Cut into thin slices and arrange in the prepared dish. (After slicing potatoes, DO NOT rinse in water; this will cause loss of the starch needed for this recipe.) Season potatoes with salt and pepper, pour cream on top and sprinkle with cheese. Bake for about 45 minutes or until crust on top is golden brown and potatoes are cooked. (See picture, page 56.)

Roesti Potatoes (Potato Pancakes)

Serves 4

600 g (21 oz) potatoes

Cook potatoes, unpeeled, for 10 minutes. Discard water and cool potatoes enough to handle. Peel the potatoes and grate on a coarse grater.

2 Tbsp butter
2 slices bacon, cut into strips
1 Tbsp finely chopped onion
Salt and pepper, to taste

Heat 1 Tbsp of the butter in a large non-stick frying pan over medium heat. Sauté bacon and onion until onion is soft. Add grated potatoes, season with salt and pepper and mix thoroughly. Using a spatula, press down on the potatoes forming them into a disk and fry for 5 minutes. Place a large plate over the potatoes, hold it with one hand and turn pan upside down. Place pan back on the stove, add remaining butter and slide in the potato disk. Fry for 5 minutes. Roesti should be golden brown.

Serving suggestion

Excellent with roast goose and any dish that has a creamy sauce.

Red Cabbage

Serves 4 to 6

500 g (1 lb) red cabbage

2 slices bacon, cut into strips
1/2 onion, sliced
1/2 Tbsp goose fat or vegetable oil
2 Tbsp red wine vinegar
125 mL (1/2 cup) chicken broth
Salt and pepper, to taste
4 Tbsp cranberry jelly

Serving suggestion

Substitute

Cut cabbage in half, remove core and shred.

In a saucepan, slowly fry bacon and onion in fat until onion is soft. Add cabbage and vinegar, stirring with a wooden spoon. Pour in broth and season with salt and pepper. Cover and simmer for 1 hour. (Make sure there is always some liquid at the bottom of the pan.) Stir in cranberry jelly before serving. (See picture, page 82.)

Excellent with roast goose, duck and hare.

For variety, in place of cranberry jelly, peel and core a large apple and cook with the cabbage.

Note: If desired, to bind liquid to cabbage, mix 1 Tbsp cornstarch with 1 Tbsp red wine and stir into steaming cabbage before serving.

Carrot Mousse

Serves 6

400 g (14 oz) carrots, peeled and coarsely chopped
2 Tbsp chopped onion
2 Tbsp butter
1 Tbsp tomato paste
125 mL (1/2 cup) whipping cream
Salt, to taste
Sugar, pinch
1 large egg
Butter (for custard cups)

Sauté onion in butter over medium heat until soft. Add carrots, tomato paste and cream; season with salt and sugar and cover. Cook until a syrupy consistency, stirring occasionally. Purée this mixture briefly in a food processor or blender, adding egg.

Preheat oven to 150°C (300°F). Brush six 100 mL (3 1/2 fl oz) custard cups with soft butter. Place cups into the freezer for a moment, then brush again with butter. (This will prevent mousse sticking to cup.) Put carrot mousse into cups filling each three-quarters full. Place cups in a shallow pan, pour warm water in the pan until it reaches one-third up the sides of the cups. Bake for 45 minutes to 1 hour. (See picture, page 18.)

Serving suggestion

Serve with any roasted meat.

Substitute

The same method and recipe can be used with peeled broccoli stems, omitting tomato paste and using a pinch of nutmeg instead of sugar.

Note: It is easier to unmold mousse if first allowed to cool for 10 minutes. Mousse can be reheated in an oven or microwave oven.

Curried Rice with Pineapple

Serves 4 to 6

2 Tbsp chopped onion
2 Tbsp butter
250 mL (1 cup) long grain rice
2 tsp curry powder
500 mL (2 cups) water
2 tsp salt
5 pineapple rings (fresh or canned)

In a saucepan, sauté onion with butter over medium heat. When onion is soft but not brown, add rice and curry; sauté for a minute. Increase heat, add water and salt, and bring to a boil. Cover and turn heat down to low. Simmer for 25 minutes, stirring the rice once towards the end of the cooking time. Cut pineapple rings into small pieces and mix into rice.

Serving suggestion

Serve with upland game birds and venison skewer.

Spaetzle

Serves 6 to 8

Spaetzle batter:
350 g (2½ cups) all-purpose flour
3 large eggs
300 mL (1¼ cups) milk
Salt and pepper, to taste
Nutmeg, pinch

Combine all the ingredients in a bowl. Using a wooden spoon, beat with a folding motion to a runny batter.

4 L (16 cups) water and 2 tsp salt (approximately)

In a large saucepan, bring salted water to a boil. Press one-third of the batter through a "Spaetzle Hobel" into boiling water (see below). Spaetzle is ready when it rises to the top. Remove with a slotted spoon and place on a baking sheet lined with a tea towel. Repeat until all batter is used.

4 Tbsp butter

When all the spaetzle has been cooked, heat 2 Tbsp of the butter in a large non-stick frying pan over medium high heat. Sauté spaetzle until it is golden brown. (Do half the quantity at a time.) Adjust seasoning with salt and pepper if necessary.

Serving suggestion

Serve with stews and pot roast.

Substitute

For variety, add 80 mL (⅓ cup) blanched and chopped spinach, or 80 mL (⅓ cup) chopped parsley to the batter.

Note: If a spaetzle hobel is not available, use a colander with large holes and press the batter through it.

An easy to use "Spaetzle Hobel"; other designs are available.

Batter should be runny but thick enough to cover spoon.

Apple Salad

Serves 6

2 large apples, Golden Delicious or Granny Smith
1/2 Tbsp lemon juice
5 Tbsp whipping cream
2 Tbsp mayonnaise
Salt, pinch
Sugar, pinch
1 tsp curry powder or dry mustard

Peel, core and cut apples into thin strips. Place in a bowl and sprinkle with lemon juice. In a separate bowl, whip the cream until it starts to thicken, then stir in mayonnaise, salt, sugar and curry powder. Add apples strips and mix. (See picture, page 56.)

Serving suggestion

Serve with game pâtés or cold game roast.

Servietten Knoedel

Serves 6

2 slices bacon, cut into strips
2 Tbsp finely chopped onion

Fry bacon and onion until onion is soft.

150 g (about 5 cups) bread cubes, cut from 2 day old white bread
1 Tbsp flour
2 Tbsp chopped parsley
1 egg
125 mL (1/2 cup) milk
Salt, pinch
Nutmeg, pinch

Place bread cubes in a large bowl and mix in flour and parsley. Beat egg with milk, salt and nutmeg, pour over bread cubes and mix thoroughly.

4 L (16 cups) water and 2 tsp salt (approximately)

In a large saucepan, bring salted water to a boil. Moisten a clean cloth napkin with cold water and lay on a flat surface. Place bread mixture on top and form a large loaf (20 cm (8 in.) long). Cover and roll loaf tightly in the napkin. Tie both ends very tightly with kitchen string. Cook in boiling water for 20 minutes. (See picture, page 64.)

Serving suggestion

Unroll and slice. Excellent with stews and pot roasts.

Note: Slices can be reheated by frying in butter.

Bread is easier to cube when partially frozen.

Sauerkraut

Serves 4 to 6

796 mL (28 fl oz) can sauerkraut

Rinse sauerkraut briefly in cold water and drain.

1 Tbsp goose fat or oil
2 slices bacon, cut into strips
1 small onion, sliced
5 juniper berries
2 bay leaves
1 medium potato
250 mL (1 cup) dry white wine
250 mL (1 cup) chicken broth

Heat fat in a saucepan over medium heat. Sauté bacon and onion until onion is soft. Add sauerkraut, juniper berries and bay leaves. Grate potato on a coarse grater over the pan and stir in wine and broth. Cover and cook gently for about 60 minutes.

Serving suggestion

Serve with roasted game birds and pork roast.

Substitute

For variety, add 125 mL (1/2 cup) diced pineapple to sauerkraut after cooking.

Potato Rolls

Serves 6

600 g (21 oz) potatoes, peeled and cut into pieces
1/2 tsp salt
1 Tbsp butter
3 egg yolks
(Potato flour if necessary)

Cook potatoes in lightly salted water. Drain water and place potatoes in a warm oven to dry for 5 to 10 minutes. Remove potatoes from oven and place in a bowl. Add salt, butter and egg yolks and mash. On a floured surface, roll potato mixture to a cylinder about 5 cm (2 in.) in diameter. Cut into 1 cm (1/2 in.) slices.

2 Tbsp butter

Heat butter in a non-stick frying pan over medium heat. Fry potato roll slices on both sides to a golden brown. (See picture, page 140.)

Serving suggestion

Excellent with game meat dishes.

For variety, add 2 Tbsp of chopped fresh chives and/or finely diced cooked ham when mashing potatoes.

Note: Use starchy potatoes for this recipe. New potatoes are not ideal since sugar in new potatoes has not converted into starch. In any case, if potato mixture is too soft add 1 or 2 Tbsp of potato flour.

DESSERTS

Chocolate Mousse

Serves 6

125 g (4 oz) semi-sweet chocolate
1 Tbsp butter
250 mL (1cup) whipping cream
2 egg whites
2 Tbsp sugar
2 Tbsp rum or coffee liqueur

Serving suggestion

Melt chocolate over boiling water or in a microwave oven, and stir in butter until blended. Whip cream with a wire whisk to soft peaks. In a separate bowl, whip egg whites and sugar with a wire whisk to soft peaks. Using a spatula, fold egg white mixture into whipped cream. Add rum and fold in chocolate.

Fill dessert dishes or leave in a bowl. Chill for 2 hours.

In dishes: Garnish with extra whipped cream and toasted almonds or chocolate shavings.

Chilled in bowl: Rinse ice cream scoop in hot water, scoop two balls onto each dessert plate and garnish with strawberries and a fresh mint leaf. (See picture below.)

Wine Sabayon with Vanilla Ice Cream and Strawberries

Serves 4

4 scoops vanilla ice cream

Sabayon:
2 egg yolks
5 Tbsp dry white wine
1 Tbsp orange liqueur
2 Tbsp sugar

8 strawberries

Scoop vanilla ice cream into deep dessert dishes and place in freezer.

Mix egg yolks, wine, orange liqueur and sugar in a medium-sized stainless steel bowl. Hold bowl over a pan of boiling water. Whip ingredients in a back and forth motion to a firm consistency. (Sabayon has to be served immediately.)

Remove ice cream from freezer. Slice and place two strawberries on each serving. (Save 4 nice slices for garnish). Spoon sabayon on top and garnish with remaining strawberry slices. (See picture below.)

Note: Sabayon can be used with hazelnut soufflé (see recipe, page 144). In this case, omit orange liqueur, ice cream and strawberries.

Hazelnut Soufflé

Serves 6

Butter and sugar for soufflé cups

Preheat oven to 190°C (375°F). Use 175 mL (¾ cup) soufflé cups. Butter and sugar the soufflé cups and set aside.

2 Tbsp unsalted butter
2 Tbsp sugar
3 heaping Tbsp flour
250 mL (1 cup) milk
2 Tbsp hazelnut liqueur
2 Tbsp hazelnuts (filberts), crushed
3 egg yolks

Soufflé base: In a bowl mix butter, sugar and flour and set aside. In a small saucepan, bring milk to a boil and whisk in the above butter mixture to thicken. Cook briefly. Remove pan from heat, add liqueur and hazelnuts, then stir in egg yolks one by one.

4 egg whites
1 Tbsp sugar

Whip the egg whites with a wire whisk or an electric beater to firm peaks, adding sugar toward the end.

Using a wire whisk, stir one-third of the whipped egg whites into soufflé base. With a rubber spatula, fold in the remainder. Pour mixture into cups until each is three-quarters full and place in a shallow pan. Just cover the bottom of the pan with warm water, place on the stove and bring water to a boil. Put in the oven for about 30 to 35 minutes. Remove soufflés, dust with icing sugar and serve immediately. (See picture below.)

Serving suggestion

At the table, poke a hole in the middle of each soufflé and put in about 1 Tbsp cranberry sauce and (optional) 2 Tbsp wine sabayon (see recipe, page 143).

Crème Caramel

Serves 6

Caramel:
150 g (3/4 cup) sugar
80 mL (1/3 cup) water

Have water ready on the side. Pour sugar into a heavy bottomed saucepan. Place on the stove over medium heat and cook to a golden caramel color. Toward the end, stir with a wooden spoon to color sugar evenly. Pour water into pan carefully (as this will create very hot steam). Bring back to a boil until water and sugar are well mixed. Pour caramel into 6 175 mL (3/4 cup) custard cups and let cool.

Custard:
500 mL (2 cups) milk
4 eggs
70 g (1/3 cup) sugar
1/2 tsp vanilla extract

Preheat oven to 150°C (300°F). In a saucepan, heat milk (do not boil) and set aside. In a large bowl, mix eggs, sugar and vanilla with a wire whisk until well blended. Stir in the hot milk, then strain through a sieve. Divide equally into custard cups.

Place custard cups in a shallow pan and pour warm water in the pan until it reaches two-thirds up the sides of the cups. Bake for about 50 minutes. Check custard by inserting a knife into the middle; if it comes out clean, the custard is cooked.

Cool the custard and place overnight in the refrigerator. When ready to serve, run a sharp knife around the edge of each custard. Turn cup upside down on a serving plate, and shake slightly to unmold. Pour any remaining caramel over the custard.

Serving suggestion

Serve plain or garnish with whipped cream and/or fruit such as strawberries, kiwi or orange sections.

Apple Strudel

Serves 6

Dough:
150 g (1 cup) all-purpose flour
1½ Tbsp vegetable oil
Salt, pinch
100 mL (3½ fl oz) lukewarm water

Mix all ingredients in a bowl, then knead well on a flat surface. If the dough sticks, add a little flour. (Dough has to be very elastic.) Shape into a ball and brush with oil or cover with plastic wrap. Place on a plate and set in a warm place for at least 30 minutes.

Filling:
1 kg (2 lbs) apples (Golden Delicious preferred)
Juice of ½ lemon
30 g (1 oz) raisins
90 g (3 oz) sugar
1 tsp cinnamon, ground

Peel, core and cut apples into 6 pieces, then cut into 3 mm (⅛ in.) slices. In a bowl, mix apples with lemon juice, raisins, sugar and cinnamon.

Assembling the Strudel: (See step-by-step pictures, page 147.)

Preheat oven to 190°C (375°F). Place linen cloth over kitchen table. (Using a table to move around makes stretching the dough easier.) Dust cloth with flour. Sprinkle the dough on all sides with flour and place in the center of the cloth. Roll out dough as thin as possible. Place floured hands, palms down, under the dough. Lifting hands slightly, move them from center to outside, stretching the dough. Remove hands and pull on dough edge to obtain a very thin 50 cm × 70 cm (20 in. × 27 in.) shape. If dough rips, overlap ripped edges and press together. Cut off thick edge all around.

6 Tbsp butter
125 mL (½ cup) dry breadcrumbs
2 Tbsp melted butter (to brush over strudel)

Melt 6 Tbsp butter in a frying pan and fry breadcrumbs for a few minutes. Sprinkle this mixture evenly over strudel dough. Then spread apple mixture over one-fourth of the dough. Roll strudel by lifting cloth, from the apple side. Place strudel on a buttered baking sheet, ends down, and brush the top with melted butter. (If baking sheet is not long enough lay out strudel in an "L" or "U" shape.) Bake for 1 hour. Brush once with butter during baking. Remove and dust with icing sugar.

Serving suggestion

Serve warm or cold with vanilla ice cream or warm vanilla sauce (see recipe, page 149).

146

Assembling the Strudel:

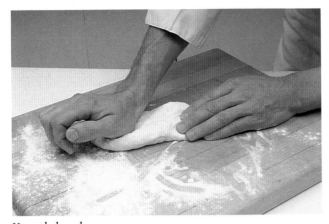
Knead dough.

Roll out.

Stretch the dough.

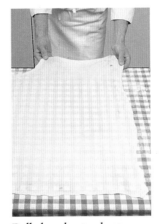
Pull dough at edges.

Roll up strudel.

Apple Strudel

147

Maple Syrup Parfait

Serves 8 to 10

250 mL (1 cup) whipped cream
3 eggs
2 Tbsp brown sugar
125 mL ($^1/_2$ cup) maple syrup

Whip cream and set aside in the refrigerator. Place eggs, sugar and maple syrup in a double boiler. Scald mixture over boiling water, stirring constantly. Remove from heat and place mixture into a bowl. Whip with an electric mixer until mixture is cool and has obtained a very firm and foamy consistency. Using a spatula, fold in the whipped cream. Pour into molds and place in the freezer for at least 5 hours before serving.

Unmold parfaits by holding molds upside down under cold running water. Then invert onto a dessert plate.

Serving suggestion

Garnish with coarsely crushed nuts, pour maple syrup over and top with whipped cream.

Note: Can be prepared days in advance. Parfait can be frozen in different shapes, sizes and molds. A loaf pan, lined with plastic wrap to help the unmolding process, can be used. Parfait tastes best when soft.

Glazed Blueberries

Serves 6

750 mL (3 cups) fresh blueberries

Vanilla Sauce:
250 mL (1 cup) milk
3 Tbsp sugar
½ tsp vanilla extract
2 tsp cornstarch
2 egg yolks

In a saucepace, bring milk (reserve 3 Tbsp for later use), sugar and vanilla to a boil. Mix cornstarch and egg yolks with the reserved milk, and whisk gradually into boiling milk. Remove pan from heat immediately and set aside.

Glaze:
125 mL (½ cup) whipping cream
1 Tbsp almond liqueur (optional)

Divide blueberries into six dessert bowls. Whip cream to soft peaks and fold with almond liqueur (if used) into vanilla sauce and pour over berries. Place under a broiler until lightly brown.

Garnish:
100 g (3½ oz) toasted almond flakes
Icing sugar, to dust

Sprinkle with toasted almonds and dust with icing sugar. (See below.)

Substitute

Strawberries or raspberries can be used.

Tarte Tatin (Turned-over Apple Pie)

Serves 6 to 8

Dough:
100 g (²/₃ cup) all-purpose flour
1 tsp baking powder
2 Tbsp sugar
70 g (¹/₃ cup) butter
1 egg yolk
1 Tbsp water

Filling:
5 to 6 large apples, Golden Delicious
50 g (¹/₄ cup) butter
100 g (²/₃ cup) sugar

Have all dough ingredients at room temperature. Place flour, baking powder and sugar into a large bowl. Cut butter into small pieces onto flour. Work, with a fork or finger tips, until almost blended. Beat egg yolk in water and mix quickly into dough. Work with hands until it forms a ball and set aside.

Peel apples, quarter and remove cores. In a 25 cm (10 in.) frying pan with a heatproof handle (or cover handle with foil), spread butter and three-quarters of the sugar evenly over the bottom. Place apple quarters, rounded side down, and overlapping slightly around the pan. (Apple quarters should be placed tightly.) Cut apple to fit in the center of the pan and sprinkle with the remaining sugar. Place pan over medium high heat until the butter and sugar turn a light amber caramel color (approximately 10 minutes). Check by lifting some of the apple quarters and moving the pan on the burner, since some areas caramelize earlier. Avoid slow cooking, as too much moisture drains from the apples and renders the caramel soupy.

Preheat the oven to 190°C (375°F). On a floured surface, knead the dough with hands and form into a disk. With a rolling pin, roll into a circle a little larger than the pan. Place over warm apples and push dough edge down. Bake in the oven for about 25 to 30 minutes or until crust is golden brown. Remove and let cool for a few minutes. Place a serving plate on top of the pan and turn pan upside down.

Serving suggestion

Serve warm with vanilla ice cream or whipped cream. (See picture below.)

Puff Pastry

300 g (2 cups) flour
150 mL (5 fl oz) water
2 tsp oil
1 Tbsp vinegar
½ tsp salt

250 g (9 oz) butter, COLD
50 g (⅓ cup) flour

Fold dough over butter square.

Press edges firmly together.

Single fold.

Double fold.

In a bowl, mix flour, water, oil, vinegar and salt until combined into a dough. Place on a floured surface and knead until smooth and shiny. Wrap dough with plastic wrap or a moist cloth and put in the refrigerator for 1 hour.

Cut butter in pieces into a bowl, add flour and work until well combined. On a floured surface, shape into a 20 cm (8 in.) square, place onto a plate and put in the refrigerator.

Place dough on a well floured surface and roll to a rectangle of 20 cm × 40 cm (8 in. × 16 in.). Place butter square on one half of the dough and fold the other half over. Press dough edges firmly together with the fingers to seal the butter into the dough. Roll dough to a thickness of about 5 mm (less than ¼ in.). Fold one-third of the dough into the center, brush off flour from top and fold the other third on top of the first. (There should now be three layers of dough – this is a 'single' fold.) Roll out dough in opposite direction. Fold both edges to meet at the center, brush off flour and fold over again to give four layers, (This is a 'double' fold.) Wrap in plastic wrap or a cloth and place dough in the refrigerator. After 1 hour, make one more single and one more double fold. Wrap dough and place back in the refrigerator for at least 1 more hour.

Pastry is now ready to use. It keeps for days in the refrigerator and can be frozen.

Cranberry Ice Cream

Serves 6 to 8

Ice cream maker is required for this recipe.

Sauce:
250 g (9 oz) cranberries, fresh
250 g (9 oz) sugar
175 mL (³/₄ cup) water

In a saucepan, bring cranberries with sugar and water to a boil. Reduce heat and boil for 5 minutes. Remove from heat and set aside to cool.

Ice cream:
1 egg
250 mL (1 cup) coffee cream
250 mL (1 cup) whipping cream

Place cranberry sauce in a blender or a food processor. Blend for a brief time, adding egg and creams while blending.

Pour into an ice cream maker, process and freeze as instructed by manufacturer.

Serving suggestion

Place 3 scoops of ice cream in each dessert dish, top with cranberry sauce (double sauce recipe when used also for topping) and a sprig of mint.

Pear Hélène
(Pear on vanilla ice cream with chocolate sauce.)

Serves 6

6 half pears (canned)
6 scoops vanilla ice cream

Chocolate sauce:
Vanilla sauce (see recipe, page 149)
100 g (3¹/₂ oz) semi-sweet chocolate

Heat vanilla sauce until almost boiling. Add chocolate and stir until chocolate is all melted; set aside.

250 mL (1 cup) whipping cream

Whip cream to soft peaks and set aside.

Divide ice cream into glass or dessert dishes. Place pear half on top of ice cream and pour chocolate sauce over pear. Garnish with whipped cream and serve immediately. (See picture, page 82.)

152

Apricot Dumplings

Serves 6

Dough:
250 mL (1 cup) milk
1 Tbsp butter
Salt, pinch
150 g (1 cup) flour
2 egg yolks

12 apricots
12 sugar cubes

4 L (16 cups) water and
1 tsp salt (approximately)

5 Tbsp butter
125 mL (½ cup) breadcrumbs (dry)
3 Tbsp sugar

Icing sugar (for garnish)

Substitute

Heat milk and butter in a saucepan over medium heat. Add salt and stir in flour with a wooden spoon. Remove pan from heat and stir until mixture loosens from the sides of pan. Let mixture cool for a few minutes and mix in egg yolks.

Slit apricots, remove stones and replace each with a sugar cube.

With floured hands, roll dough on a floured surface into a cylinder shape of 50 mm (2 in.) diameter. Cut cylinder into 12 slices and cover each apricot with one slice of dough.

In a large saucepan, bring salted water to a boil. Drop dumplings in water and simmer for 12 minutes. Remove dumplings with a slotted spoon and dry on a paper towel.

Melt butter in a frying pan over medium heat and fry breadcrumbs and sugar briefly. Roll dumplings one by one in this mixture. Dust with icing sugar when serving. (See below.)

Plums (do not add sugar cubes).

Apricot dumplings.

HANDLING, BUTCHERING AND MEAT PREPARATION

BUTCHERING

Table of Contents

HANDLING GAME ANIMALS

Many factors can influence the flavor of game meat. The flavor can be light and delicate or heavy and strong. Understanding these factors, which contribute to the final product, will help to get the best of the meat.

Behavior

During and a few weeks after the rutting season, the meat of males from the deer family (deer, reindeer, elk and moose) is usually tough and has a strong flavor, and their livers are inedible.

When field dressing these animals, it is absolutely essential to avoid tainting the meat with the secretions from the musk glands which are easily visible on the inside of the hind leg knees. One knife should be used for removing the glands and another for field dressing. To remove them, cut well outside the glands, and avoid touching them with your hands, or remove them after you have field dressed the animal.

Rutting animals should be skinned before aging the flesh of the animal. Despite the best handling and preparation, such animals will yield few prime cuts. Most of the meat should be used for braising and stewing, after marinating with a red wine marinade, or for grinding and sausage making. Tenderloin and loin are generally tender enough for steaks and also top sirloin and inside round from the hind leg may still yield choice cuts. Check for tenderness after aging by pressing cuts of meat with the finger; if it breaks through quite easily, the meat is suitable for steaks, schnitzels or roasts.

Method of taking

After sighting an animal, before shooting, consider the following: Where is the animal? Can you easily get it out in good condition and in a reasonable amount of time?

A quick clean kill is fair to the animal and yields the best meat for the table. The ideal shot is right through the shoulder blade on a relaxed animal, piercing lungs and heart and quickly draining the animal of blood. A chased, wounded or otherwise stressed animal experiences changes in its body chemistry and muscle tone which make its meat tougher and stronger tasting then a relaxed animal. If the blood is not drained properly, the meat will spoil quickly. Such animals should be skinned as soon as possible and aged only briefly.

Handling in the field

If possible, hunt in cold weather. It is important to quickly cool the freshly downed animal by field dressing it immediately, since bacterial decay occurs rapidly in a warm body cavity. The cavity should be opened fully, including the throat, unless a trophy cape is required, to permit complete air circulation. The carcass should be removed from the field as soon as possible, or if removal is delayed, moved to a shady spot with the cavity propped open for cooling.

If remaining in a hunting camp in warm weather, hang the animal or quarters in a cool breezy place covered with loose cheesecloth to keep insects away. Despite these precautions, taking large game in warm weather is not ideal. Under such circumstances, quick removal to a cool hanging place is recommended.

From the cook's point of view, taking the animal out whole allows for the maximum choice of cuts. For large animals such as elk and moose, however, it is far more practical to quarter them.

At all stages keep the meat dry and as clean of hair and dirt as possible. If the meat gets dirty, wipe with a clean cloth or wait until clean tap water is available and wash with a moist cloth and wipe dry. Using water in the field could introduce bacteria.

Aging

All animals should be aged in a cool, insect-free place. If whole, the animal should be hung from its hind legs while aging, in order to drain blood from choice cuts. Heart and liver should be eaten as fresh as possible or immediately frozen.

Aging is a chemical process in which enzymes break down the connective tissues, tenderize the meat and improve the flavor. Temperature is critical in this process. Constant 1° to 3°C (34° to 38°F) temperatures are ideal; colder temperatures hinder the aging process, warmer temperatures accelerate it and encourage unwanted bacterial decay. Meat does not age when frozen. If an animal must be aged at temperatures varying from the ideal, aging times must be adjusted accordingly. (Aging times are dealt with in the chapter of individual animal.)

Leaving hide on, during aging, will protect the meat from drying out, moderate the effect of temperature fluctuation and prevent insect damage. However, large animals with a thick hide, such as moose, should be skinned before aging to speed cooling. Also, remove hide from rutting animals since skin would taint the meat.

Generally, larger and older animals require more aging than smaller and younger ones. Rutting or post-rutting animals also require longer aging. However, it is important not to over-age animals.

Butchering and Meat Preparation

Special care must be taken to remove all the fat and the bones, which are strongly flavored and will impart a gamy taste to the meat. The fat in game animals is not marbled through the meat fibre as it is in domestic meats. It covers the outside of the meat which makes it simple to remove. The trimming of silver skin and ligaments will improve the tenderness of the meat. Separating the meat into different muscle groups will ensure consistent tenderness in each cut.

Basic equipment needed for butchering: A cool, clean place and a large disinfected cutting surface are necessary to reduce the chance of bacterial growth. Sharp boning and cutting knives are easier and safer to work with; less pressure is needed therefore the knifes are easier to control. Also required are a sharpening stone, meat saw, freezer paper, tape, marking pen, string and a helpful person to assist in the cutting and wrapping of the meat.

Freezing: Due to the high water and low fat content of most game meat, it is ideal for freezing. Game meats can be kept frozen for up to one year. When cutting and wrapping portions, bear in mind serving plans and tightly wrap each piece in brown freezer paper, waxed one side. Seal it with tape, label and date the contents for future reference.

Equipment needed for butchering: Boning knife (1), cutting knife (2), sharpening steel (3), meat saw (4), freezer paper (5), tape (6), marking pen (7) and string (8).

Sharpen your knife often. Hold knife blade at 45° towards sharpening steel and draw knife in an arc from base to tip. Repeat on other side and continue until knife is sharp.

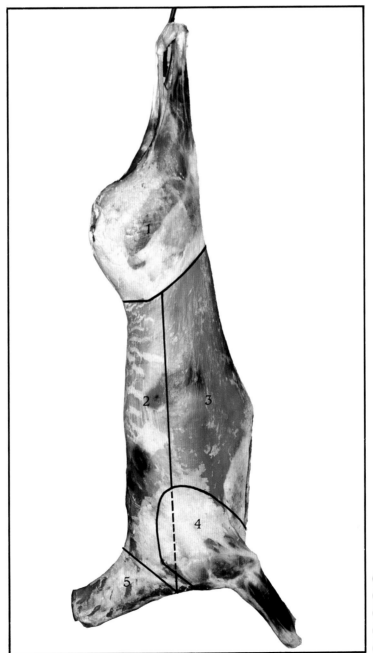

(1) Hind leg
(2) Saddle
(3) Ribs
(4) Shoulder
(5) Neck

SEPARATING INTO MAJOR PARTS (shown on deer). Same method applies for sheep, antelope, bear and boar.

To remove hind legs: Saw between hind legs and loin. Then separate the two legs by sawing through the middle of tail-bone.

To remove shoulder: First mark the shoulder with a shallow cut at the base of the neck and just behind the shoulder blade.

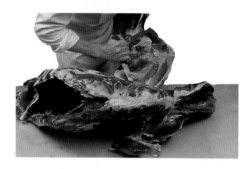

Pull shoulder towards you and start cutting from rib cage following the natural seam, until the end of the shoulder blade; then remove. Repeat for the other shoulder.

To remove ribs: Saw off ribs about 3 cm (1¼ in.) away from the loin. Repeat on the other side.

To separate neck from saddle: cut along the third rib. Neck meat can be used for stews, sausages or ground.

When deboning:
a) Use sharp boning or hunting knife.
b) Always cut with the tip of the knife, keeping blade at a slight angle to the bone in order to remove as much meat as possible.

DEBONING LEG (hind leg) (shown on deer)

Trim off surface fat and silver skin before deboning the leg. Trimming at this stage is easier, since bones keep the meat stretched.

Removing hip-bone and tail-bone: Pull away bone with one hand while the other is cutting meat with knife blade close to the bone. Once the ball joint is loosened, the hip-bone and tail-bone will be easy to remove.

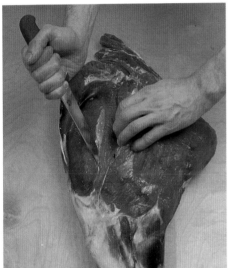

Cut along second seam with knife point until knee-bone is reached. Carefully cut meat away on each side of the bone.

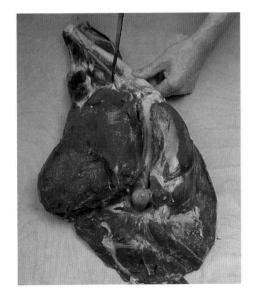

Cut meat away along each side of the leg-bone. Turn leg around end for end. Start cutting underneath the leg-bone at foot end (so leg bone can be grasped), pull bone up towards you and continue to scrape underneath until leg-bone is completely free, then continue and free knee-bone. (On larger animals — such as moose and elk — for easier leg deboning, separate knee-bone and leg-bone at the joint and pull out leg-bone toward the foot.)

Cutting meat from hind leg into the different muscle groups: Always follow the natural seams, pulling meat away with one hand while cutting with the other.

First remove inside (top) round (1).

Remove shank (2).

Separate round and top sirloin from outside (bottom) round (3) and eye of round (4).

Cut top sirloin (5) from round (6). When all muscle groups have been separated, trim off ligaments and silver skin.

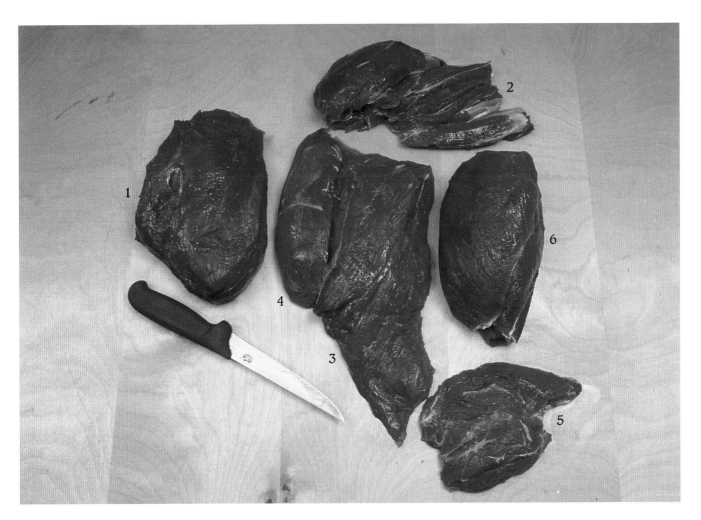

Cuts from leg:

Inside (top) round (1): Can be used as a roast or cut into steaks, medallions, schnitzels, piccatas or cubed for skewers.

Shank (2): Use like other trimmings, for stew, sausages or ground.

Outside (bottom) round (3) **with eye of round** (4): Usually left together on small animals but are separated on large animals like moose and elk. Outside (bottom) round and eye of round are coarsely grained and, therefore, tougher than the other parts of the leg, but are excellent for braising (pot roast).

Top sirloin (5): Use as directed for inside (top) round. Top sirloin is very juicy and tender.

Round (6): Best used as a roast or cut into schnitzels and piccatas.

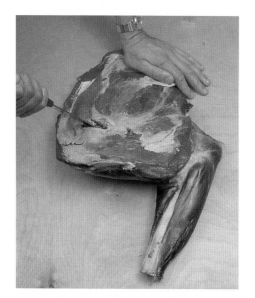

DEBONING SHOULDER (front leg) (shown on deer)

Loosen the ball-socket joint and remove meat on top of shoulder blade. Cut along each side of this bone with the tip of your knife.

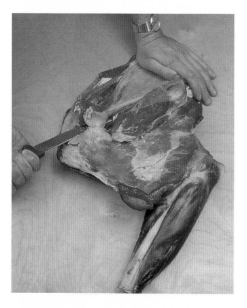

Press down at the end of shoulder blade and cut underneath the socket joint very close to the bone (so shoulder blade can be grasped). Pull blade toward you while scraping meat underneath.

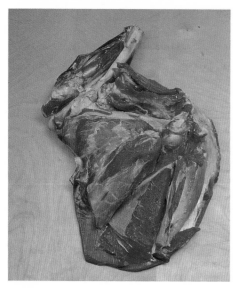

Cut along each side of knee-bone and leg-bone. Turn meat around end for end.

Start cutting underneath the leg-bone at foot end (so leg-bone can be grasped), pull up bone toward you and continue to scrape underneath until leg-bone is completely free, then continue and free knee-bone. (On larger animals — such as moose and elk — for easier leg deboning, separate knee-bone and leg-bone at the joint and pull out leg-bone toward the foot.)

Deboned trimmed shoulder: Can be used for braising (pot roast), stew, ground and sausages. Shoulder from a young animal can be braised whole. (With large animals — such as moose and elk — cut into 3 pieces along the seams for braising.)

REMOVING OUTER SKIN FROM BIG GAME LIVER

Outer skin on big game liver becomes tough when cooked.

Make a shallow cut at the thick end of liver. With one hand grasp and pull the skin while using thumb to separate skin from liver.

TRIMMING SADDLE (shown on deer)

Tenderloins are the inside loins. They can be roasted whole or cut into medallions, steaks or flakes. Tenderloins should be removed after a few days of aging to prevent them from drying out.

Removing silver skin on saddle: Hold skin taut while cutting underneath, holding knife blade at an angle towards the skin.

Cuts from the saddle:

Saddle (1): Can be cut in two or three pieces. Or cut into loins, racks or chops.

Loin (2): To remove loins, cut down close to the back-bone to ribs, pulling meat while cutting loin along the ribs. Serve as roast or cut into steaks, medallions (5) or flakes.

Rack (3): Cut meat on each side of the back-bone to ribs. Then saw off back-bone. Portion, and remove meat from between ribs.

Chops (4): Cut rack between each rib-bone.

CARVING SADDLE FROM DEER, ANTELOPE OR SHEEP
(shown on antelope)

Carve the saddle in front of guests or cut it in the kitchen and place meat back on the bone after carving.

Cut down on one side close to the back-bone and the ribs.

Then continue to cut, following close to the bone until meat is free.

Slice meat at an angle and place back over the bone.

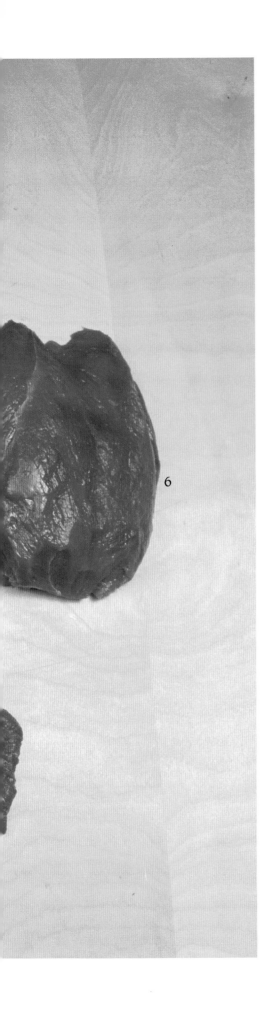

6

Wrap meat as air tight as possible. Write species and meat cut with quantity and year.

Meat cuts: (used in this book)

Saddle (1), loin (2), rack (3), chops (4), medallions (5), roast (6), steak (7), schnitzel (8) and piccatas (9).

SEPARATING INTO MAJOR PARTS (only for large animals) (shown on elk)

Unlike deer, large animals — such as moose and elk — are split in half and cut into quarters between the second and third rib. (Leg and shoulder are deboned the same way as the deer unless otherwise stated.) Separating the animal and deboning the loin section, which is different from the deer, is shown below.

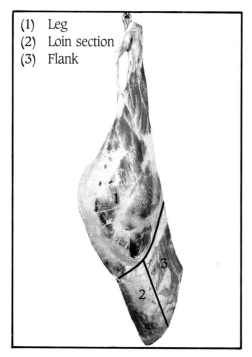

(1) Leg
(2) Loin section
(3) Flank

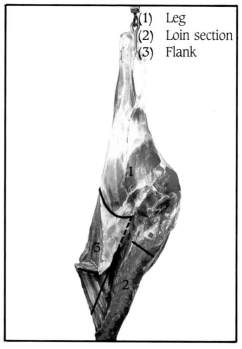

(1) Leg
(2) Loin section
(3) Flank

SEPARATING HIND QUARTER (Outside view.)　　　　　(Inside view.)

Hang hind quarter as shown. **To remove flank:** cut around the top of the leg to within 3 cm (1¼ in.) of the loin, then cut down in a straight line to the ribs and saw through ribs.

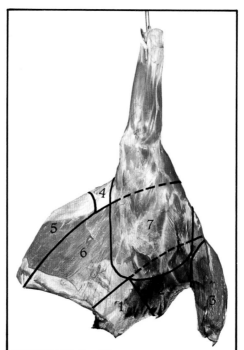

(1) Rib eye
(2) Chuck
(3) Neck
(4) Brisket
(5) Breast
(6) Ribs
(7) Shoulder

SEPARATING FRONT QUARTER

Hang front quarter as shown. To remove shoulder, start cutting at the base of the brisket, cutting down between shoulder and rib cage following the natural seam. The weight of the rib cage will assist the cutting. Cut off shoulder at the end of the shoulder blade.

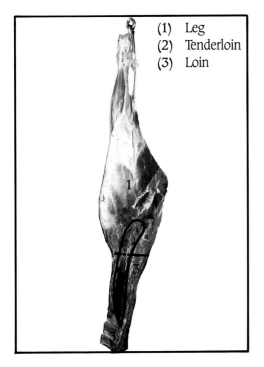

(1) Leg
(2) Tenderloin
(3) Loin

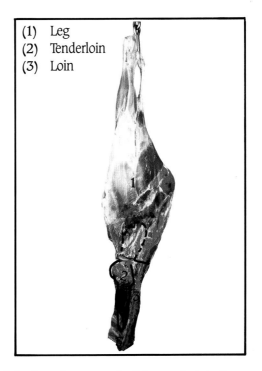

(1) Leg
(2) Tenderloin
(3) Loin

To remove loin section (tenderloin and loin): On the inside of the leg, the top end of the tenderloin lies over the hip-bone. In order to remove the tenderloin whole, strip the tenderloin from the hip-bone (as shown with dotted line) and fold it down toward ribs. Separate loin section from leg at the end of the hip-bone, leaving tenderloin and loin intact.

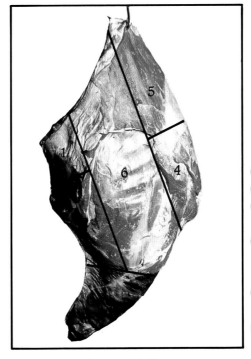

(1) Rib eye: Roast
(2) Chuck: Pot Roast
(3) Neck: Stew, Sausage and Ground
(4) Brisket: Can be used for Broth, Stew, Sausage and Ground
(5) Breast: Ground, Sausage and Stew
(6) Ribs: Sausage and Ground

Remove meat from the rib cage, then cut meat (as shown with lines).

DEBONING LOIN SECTION (ONLY ELK and MOOSE)
(shown on elk)

To remove the tenderloin, cut very close along the back-bone, then while pulling meat, continue cutting along the ribs until the tenderloin is free.

On the other side of the back-bone is the loin which may be removed using the same method as for the tenderloin. With the loin, it is easier to begin at the ribs.

Tenderloin (the smaller piece) and loin trimmed of silver skin: Can be left whole for special occasions or cut into steaks.

LARDING

Pot roast will benefit from larding with pork fat. Larding keeps the meat juicy and makes a good flavor combination. Carrots will also give flavor but mainly make the roast look appetizing. Pork fat and carrots should be cut into pencil-sized pieces. To push fat and carrots into meat, a larding needle or a knife with a narrow blade can be used. When using a knife to make holes, pork fat must be frozen after cutting to size, so that it can be pushed into the meat.

CUTTING RABBIT OR HARE INTO PIECES (shown on rabbit).

Rabbit and hare are seldom roasted whole because the hind legs need longer cooking time than the saddle (back). Ribs and shoulders are used for stock unless rabbit or hare is cut into pieces and breaded or braised.

Remove hind legs by cutting down on the side of hip-bone to ball joint. Bend leg out so ball will pop out of socket. Cut through joint and remove leg.

To remove shoulder section, cut between rib cage and shoulder.

Chop ribs in a straight line from the base of neck along the side of the loins. (Poultry shears can be used.) The piece that is left is the untrimmed saddle. From this, trim the hip-bones and neck.

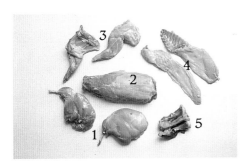

Rabbit pieces: legs (1), saddle (2), shoulders (3), ribs (4) and hip-bones (5). For braising, legs can be cut again at the knee and saddle can be chopped in 3 or 4 pieces, depending on size.

The saddle consists of 2 loins lying on either side of the back-bone. They can be removed by cutting very closely along the back-bone.

HANDLING GAME BIRDS

HANDLING GAME BIRDS

The preparation and cooking of game birds will depend on their size, diet, age and if they were plucked or skinned. For example, a blue grouse feeding on September berries is a delicacy and need only be plucked. The same bird feeding later on conifer needles needs to have its strong tasting skin removed. When dealing with waterfowl, the preparation will depend on the degree of sloughy or fishy odor of the bird. The flavor of ducks feeding on grain fields is worlds apart from slough feeding and fish eating ones.

AGE and SEX

A young bird can be identified by its smaller size. Its plumage is more immature and can include pin feathers. Also, the breast-bone is moveable and the beak and feet are soft. The male is distinguished by a more colorful plumage and in the turkey and pheasant the size of the spurs determine age. The female generally has a finer textured meat and is more tender.

CLEANING

All game birds should be cleaned immediately, but in below freezing weather this can be postponed until the end of the day. However, do not store them in plastic bags.

The cleaning of birds is quite simple. Begin by plucking a thin strip of feathers from the tail up to the breast-bone. Make a very shallow cut, taking care not to rupture any intestines in the process. Insert one to three fingers into this cavity and carefully pull out the organs. This may also be done very neatly with a bird-gutting knife, a tool resembling a button hook.

In upland birds the crop should also be removed. The crop is a food sac which lies between the neck and breast.

AGING

As with all game meats, aging will tenderize the meat making it easy to digest and, improve its flavor.

Upland birds such as wild turkey, pheasant, grouse, partridge and quail should be hung by the neck and aged for about three days in a cool, airy place such as a cold room or cellar. The feathers should be left on while aging to prevent skin from drying out. Herbs such as thyme, rosemary or tarragon can be stuffed into the body cavity during the aging process.

Water fowl should be aged after plucking. Place them in the refrigerator for about three days before cooking or freezing.

PLUCKING

Unless it is badly shot, very old or very sloughy and destined for the stewing pot, birds should always be plucked, not skinned. When plucking in the field, which is easier since bird is still warm, game regulations may require that a complete wing be left intact for identification.

Upland birds are best dry plucked because their skin is more fragile than water fowl. Birds can be also immersed in hot water, for a short period, to facilitate the plucking.

Water fowl should be plucked before aging, so the feathers will not taint the meat; sometimes feathers can harbor small insects and may smell sloughy. If the birds are plucked at home the process is made easier and faster by rough plucking first, then hold the hind legs and dip the bird into simmering water to which paraffin or plucking wax may be added. The wax, together with the fine feathers is then peeled off leaving the skin intact. Any remaining downy feathers can be singed with a candle or gas flame, taking care to avoid burning the skin. Freshly plucked birds should then be rinsed in cold water and dried before storing or cooking.

SKINNING

The skin of all birds with its underlying fat layer will prevent the meat from drying out. The skin is essential in roasting and will produce a much more delicious meal.

If it is absolutely necessary to skin the bird, begin by cutting off the wings and feet, then slit from the top of the breast-bone down to the tail. Strip the skin from the breast and back; then pull in down over the legs as though removing socks. The bird should now be totally skinned. Remove the neck and tail.

MARINATING

Strong flavors, on waterfowl and grouse, may be moderated by marinating the bird in milk for one to two days in the refrigerator. Juniper berries, peppercorns, bay leaves, thyme or rosemary added to the marinade will improve the flavor and impart an interesting taste to the meat.

COOKING

The meat of game birds has less fat than domestic ones, more basting is required to keep the meat moist. In general, birds should be cooked until the breast meat is just a little pink. When roasting, a young bird is best, while old birds are better braised, stewed or used in pâtés, terrines or pies.

TYING UPLAND BIRDS (shown on pheasant)

Legs from upland birds are very loose; they should be tied for roasting. This will make birds easy to handle and give them a desirable shape.

If not already done, remove wings. Push legs down, pressing together so breasts will come up.

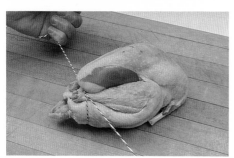

Lay kitchen string underneath the back-bone and tie legs to body with a knot.

Holding string taut, bring to the front of the bird and make a double knot between breasts and neck.

COOKING BIRD (shown on pheasant)

When turning a bird in frying or roasting pan, never poke a fork into breast meat (juices would leak out). Either go between breast and leg, or

use meat tongs.

Hold bird with a fork between breast and leg; if juices coming out of cavity are clear, the bird is cooked. If they are slightly pink, return to the oven for a few more minutes.

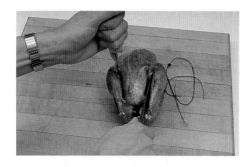

Remove string. Hold bird with a fork between leg and breast.

Cut between breast and leg to leg joint; push leg away from body so joint will pop open. Cut off leg, then remove the other leg. (If legs show any pink, place them back in pan and cook a few more minutes.)

Removing breasts: Cut close to the breast-bone towards wish-bone and down to the wing joint. Loosen joint with the tip of the knife, then cut breast off — always point knife slightly towards bones to get the most meat possible. Remove second breast.

Slice breasts on an angle and cut legs in half at the joint.

178

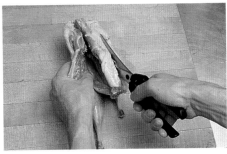

CUTTING UP A BIRD (shown on pheasant)

This method will leave some bones with the meat, keeping the meat juicy and giving more flavor to a sauce.

Remove back-bone by cutting along each side using poultry shears, a knife or cleaver.

Split bird down the middle between the breasts. Small birds, up to partridge size, can be left in halves; larger birds can be divided further.

Cut off legs from breasts and chop both breasts and legs in half. Breast from a goose may be chopped into 3 or 4 pieces.

TRIMMING LIVER OF BIRD

Veins in the inside of bird livers are sometimes bitter. Hold veins with one hand; at the same time slide the knife down the veins and push the liver away.

(shown on pheasant)

Remove leg by cutting down between leg and breast to the joint.

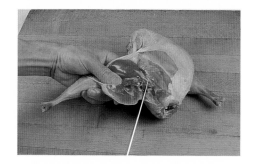

Bend leg out so ball joint will pop out. Cut through remaining meat to remove leg. Remove other leg.

To remove breasts, cut close to the breast-bone towards wish-bone and down to the wing joint. Loosen joint, using the tip of the knife.

Lay bird on its side and pull out breast away from the joint, assisting with the knife. Cut close to bone to ensure tenderloin remains with breasts. Remove second breast.

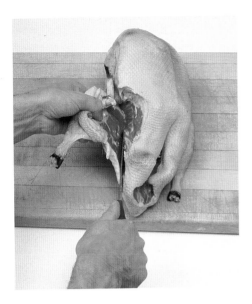

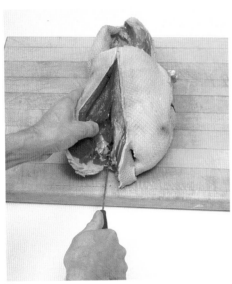

REMOVING LEGS AND BREASTS FROM WATER FOWL
(shown on goose)

Water fowl can be cut the same way as other birds. Leg and wing joints are tighter and breasts are longer.

To remove legs and breasts, see directions and pictures on pheasant. (See pictures opposite)

On left, goose breast skin removed and wrapped in bacon (can also be cut into medallions or piccatas). Ends of bacon should meet underneath breasts so they won't unfold during roasting. On right, skin is left on to protect breast from drying out during roasting.

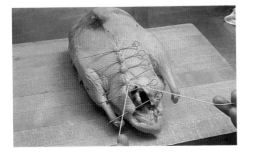

CLOSING CAVITY OF STUFFED BIRD (shown on goose)

Use small skewers or toothpicks and kitchen string.

181

First remove skin by pulling with one hand while assisting with the other and/or a knife.

Remove breast from carcass, then cut off the wing-bone.

Peel off the tenderloin, assisting with the knife.

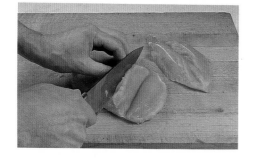

Cut tenderloin horizontally through the middle to within 3 mm (1/8 in.) of the other side (do not cut through completely). Leave attached and open like a butterfly.

Start to cut at the thick end of breast. On small breast make butterfly cut (one cut incomplete, one complete) to get large portions

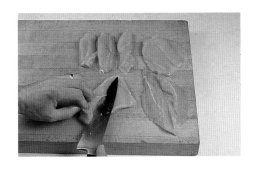

At thin end of breast cut wider slices to make equal portions.

Pound schnitzels.

Fold ham and cheese into schnitzels. (Cordon Bleu)

183

STUFFING BREASTS (shown on pheasant)

Open breast by unfolding the tenderloin.

Make an incomplete cut at the thick part of breast from center toward outside edge.

Pipe filling down on the center of the breast.

Close by first folding back the incomplete cut, then overlap with the tenderloin.

DEBONING BIRD FROM THE BACK (shown on duck)

With a delicious stuffing, a bird deboned from the back makes an excellent roast which is easy to slice after roasting. Use carcass from bird(s) for stock or soup. All birds can be deboned from the BACK (try first on a chicken because it is easier to debone than a game bird). All that is needed is a sharp boning knife.

Cut skin from neck to tail along the back-bone.

Cut through wing joint leaving shoulder bone on the carcass. Loosen meat with the tip of the knife, cutting towards leg.

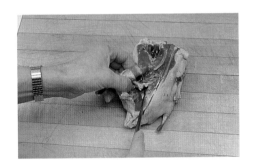

Loosen meat half way around leg joint. Hold leg-bone with one hand cut connective tendons in joint with the knife. Leg is now free from carcass.

Cut meat towards the breast-bone holding knife blade towards the bone.

185

Scrape meat free to the edge of breast-bone. (Meat is still attached at point of breast bone.) Do the same on the other side of bird.

Pull off carcass starting at neck end holding meat down with the knife.

Remove thigh-bones from the legs, cutting them off at the joint.

Fold tenderloin of breasts towards the legs to distribute meat evenly. Trim all loose skin from around bird.

Place stuffing in the middle. Fold meat over so sides overlap slightly.

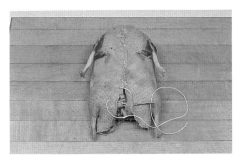

Sew bird together starting at the breast, using a darning needle and kitchen string.

Roasted duck: First remove string, cut behind where wing-bones are attached to meat, then cut this piece in half. Slice the remaining bird; legs can be removed if desired.

Different methods to prevent quails from opening while cooking.

187

GLOSSARY

Baste:	Brush or pour melted fat, butter or meat juices over (meat) while roasting. Meat is basted to keep it from drying out.
Beef Middle:	Large, treated intestine of cattle used as sausage casing. (See Casing.)
Braise:	Brown meat quickly and then cook slowly with a little liquid, in a covered pan, until done.
Brisket:	The cut of meat from the breast of an animal.
Casing:	Tube into which sausage meat is stuffed. Casing may be fibrous or synthetic (man-made) or natural (treated intestine of pork, beef or lamb).
Chop:	Meat cutlet from loin with rib bone in.
Coffee cream:	Cream which contains only 10 per cent fat.
Curdle:	Separation which occurs when cream added to a sauce is reduced too much.
Cure (Saltpeter may be used):	Salt mixed with sodium nitrate; used for curing meat. Beside giving sausages a nice pink color, it will prevent the growth of bacteria. (Can be bought in a butcher shop or a butcher supply shop.) (If saltpeter is used, follow directions on package.)
Deglaze:	Dilution of the concentrated juices in a pan in which meat has been roasted, braised or fried. For this purpose, white, red wine, Madeira or some other heavy wine is brought to the boil in the pan while stirring constantly. Water, clear soup, stock and sometimes cream can be used instead of wine.
Dijon mustard:	Mustard which originally was made in Dijon, a town in France.
Dumpling (Quenelle or Knoedel):	Small round or oval shape of meat, dough or bread mixture usually boiled or baked.
Flake (émincés):	Small, thin pieces of meat sliced from a tender cut.
Forcemeat:	Fine delicate ground meat mixture used for pâté and stuffing.
Glaze:	To coat fruits, vegetables or meat with a syrup or to pour a sauce over and brown under a broiler.
Grill:	Cook on a hot metal rack like a barbecue.

Hazelnut (Filbert):	The fruit of the hazelnut. Cultivated hazelnuts are called filberts.
Juniper Berries:	Berries of a bush which grows wild in woods and mountain gullies. Used to flavor marinade. They are also used as seasoning with certain foods especially with game. (Available in specialty food stores.)
Knoedel:	German word for dumpling. (See Dumpling.)
Lard:	To thread strips of white and firm pork fat into large cuts of lean meat, using a larding-needle or knife.
Link (sausage):	After stuffing, to twist sausage in portion size.
Mallet:	Hammer having a wooden or soft metal head used for pounding meat.
Marinade:	Certain liquids (such as wine, oil, milk or buttermilk) mixed with herbs in which meat is soaked to alter flavor before being cooked. Marinade is usually used with old or strongly flavored meat.
Medallion:	Meat from loin or leg cut in the shape of a medallion, round or oval.
Mousse:	**Dessert:** Normally made with whipped cream and/or gelatin. **Vegetable:** Purée of vegetables, with whipping cream and/or whipped egg whites added.
Piccatas:	Thin cutlets from tender part of hip or loin.
Poach:	To cook in liquid that is not quite boiling.
Quenelles:	French word for dumpling. (See Dumpling.)
Raw sugar (Demerara):	Partially refined sugar. When further refined, becomes white granulated sugar.
Reduce:	To boil down the volume of a liquid by evaporation, particularly a sauce. Reducing increases flavor and also thickens sauces.
Roesti:	Potato pancake.

Saddle:	Part of the hind quarters extending from the ribs to the leg on both sides.
Sauté:	To fry quickly or brown in little fat or oil.
Scald:	To bring a liquid to a temperature just below the boiling point.
Seam:	In meat, an obvious division which occurs where silver lining separates muscle from muscle.
Schnitzel:	Escallop (thin cutlet) sometimes coated with egg and breadcrumbs and cooked in butter or fat.
Servietten Knoedel:	Bread dumpling mixture rolled in a napkin and poached in salted water.
Simmer:	To keep at, or just below, the boiling point.
Skim:	To remove all the scum from the surface of a stock, sauce or stew, using a large spoon.
Slotted spoon:	Large spoon with small holes.
Spaetzle:	Egg batter cooked in boiling water, drained and sautéed in butter.
Spaetzle Hobel:	Utensil used to prepare spaetzle.
Stuffer:	Utensil used for forcing sausage meat into casing.
Suet:	The hard fat about the kidneys and loins of cattle.
Water bath (bain-marie):	Pan partially filled with water to regulate heat evenly during baking.
Wood mushrooms:	Mushrooms found in the forest — bolets, chanterelles and morels. If wood mushrooms are not available, use regular mushrooms.

INDEX

An "*" indicates that other game meat can be used.

194

T

U

V

W

ADDITIONAL COPIES

To order additional copies of "GAME. The Art of Preparation
and Cooking of Game and Game Fowl", send $24.95 plus $2.50 for
postage and handling (total of $27.45 per copy) plus tax where applicable, to:

N and C Publishing
P.O. Box 78062, H.P.O.
Calgary, Alberta, T2H 2Y1

Make personal cheque or money order to
N and C PUBLISHING.
(Please print your name and address clearly for return mail..)